Successful Training Practice

Human Resource Management in Action

Series editor: Brian Towers

Successful Training Practice

A Manager's Guide to Personnel Development

Alan H. Anderson

First published 1993

Blackwell Publishers
108 Cowley Road
Oxford   OX4 1JF
UK

238 Main Street, Suite 501
Cambridge, Massachusetts 02142
USA

British Library Cataloguing in Publication Data
A CIP catalogue record for this book is available from the British Library.

Library of Congress Cataloging-in-Publication Data
Anderson, Alan H., 1950–
     Successful training practice: a manager's guide to personnel
  development / Alan H. Anderson.
          p.   cm. — (Human resource management in action)
     Includes bibliographical references and index.
     ISBN 0–631–18766–9 (pbk.)
     1. Employee—Training of.   2. Supervision of employees.
  I. Title.   II. Series.
  HF5549.5.T7A63   1992
  658.3'124—dc20   92–17012
                                                              CIP

Typeset in 11 on 13 pt Plantin
by Graphicraft Typesetters Ltd, Hong Kong
Printed in Great Britain by TJ Press, Padstow, Cornwall

This book is printed on acid-free paper

This book is dedicated to Evelyn Sharp

Contents

Figures

Tables and exhibits

Acknowledgements

I would like to thank Anna Hayward for doing some of the typing and Professor Tom Reeves for allowing me some time to write. Much of the material comes from the consultancy firm, Anderson Associates, Personnel and Management Advisors, based in Melbourn, Herts, England, so an acknowledgement is warranted. Thanks go to Sally Vince for adapting my shorthand style, and to Richard Burton of Blackwell Publishers.

My special thanks go to Maureen, Ross and Kerry for all their hard work and for coping with me while I wrote this book.

Foreword

The performance of the British economy continues to disappoint as it has done for more than a century, relative to its rivals. Some part of the explanation lies in economic management but another, and perhaps the most important, lies in what is taking place in the boardroom, office and workshop. The record of British companies is not uniformly depressing – there are still some stars – but average performance continues to cause concern. Within companies many see the problem in training or, more precisely, its deficiency in both quality and quantity. It is notoriously difficult to make such comparisons between countries but the evidence is mounting that British managers, relative to their German, French or Japanese counterparts, give low priority and resources to all forms of training, including their own. It is also probable that the superior training record in other countries is more than accidentally associated with the consistently higher performance of their economies and their companies. Government over the past twenty years has, in fairness, recognized this deficiency but, so far, has had little to show for the efforts and resources expended and there is always the continuing temptation to rein back training expenditure to meet immediate problems and needs – as seen in the cuts imposed on the latest agents of training initiatives, the training and enterprise councils.

Where all this really hurts is at the place of work, since a low commitment to training can give negative signals to employees. A change in attitude can make all the difference and bring positive human resource benefits. As Sisson puts it:

> ... if the organization is seen by its employees to be investing in training and development the message that it views people as the most important resource is likely to be taken seriously ... by

contrast, the organization that does little training and development would appear to have far greater difficulty in convincing employees of the seriousness of its commitment and hence in winning their loyalty. *Personnel Management in Britain*, Blackwell, 1989, pp. 34–5.

It is in this context that Alan Anderson's book is such a valuable addition to the training library. In the spirit of war being too important to be left to the generals he argues that training is not simply the responsibility of training departments but also line managers. This book is written primarily for them: an 'how-to-do-it' book covering manual worker, supervisory and management training, and giving precise and practical guidance from the design and development of training programmes through to their implementation, evaluation and audit.

Yet, in meeting the needs of practical people Alan Anderson brings together valuable experience in personnel, training and consultancy as well as the insights of his academic work. All this gives the book credibility in business schools, colleges and the place of work. Training needs a better image and expert professionalism. This book will contribute to both.

Brian Towers
Strathclyde Business School

Introduction

Whose job is it to ensure that people in organisations have the guidance and help they need to develop their talents? Until a decade ago, the answer in many large companies and government departments would have been the personnel and training sections.

Managers had little control over who worked for them or what training these people received. Not surprisingly, many managers abdicated their responsibility to encourage promising staff.

Things are changing, and the personnel and training department is going through its own version of glasnost, an important part of which is persuading managers to take back their development responsibilities.

D. Clutterbuck
'Managers answer the call for workforce training'

Themes and the Audience

The main theme of this book is that line managers with a responsibility for people must have some 'ownership' of both training and development.[1] For too long training has been in the hands of specialist training advisers, or support staff, who have tended to usurp the line executive with their specialist knowledge and people skills.[2] In addition, the line manager, seen as an executive in the main chain of command from chief executive to supervisor, has suffered from another 'ownership' claim not covered by the quote above from Clutterbuck. The emphasis, of late, has been on the learner.[3] It is the learner's style and level of participation that has dominated textbooks. Student-centred learning and self-development are the 'in things' in training. There is a strong case for emphasizing the role of learner, but we should not neglect, or indeed negate, the other factors contributing to work-based learning. Indeed, in this book it is proposed that a system is used to analyse training covering many variables in addition to the learner orientation or approach. Further, this system should be managed ultimately by the line manager with input and support from the specialist. Hence the key themes of the book are:

1 The line manager is so responsible for training that he or she is a line trainer.
2 The learner is important, but is only part of the overall training system which we should use as our frame of reference.

The traditional approach to a system of training tends to cover four phases:

1 A *training needs* analysis.
2 A *design/development* stage.
3 An *implementation* stage.
4 Some form of *evaluation* which feeds back into a new or revised phase of redefining training needs.

The system has a roll-on effect moving on to redesign etc. after the needs have been re-examined.

This traditional approach has been modified,[4] with phases superimposed upon one another, qualified with a list of 'contingency variables' depending upon given circumstances of organizations, and indeed challenged by others as being too static and mechanistic. This discussion will be followed up later, but suffice to say at this stage this traditional four-phased approach is a useful starting point for its simplicity if nothing else. It also provides a useful 'demarcation zone' between the responsibilities of line and staff managers for training which we can use.

In this book, the activities of putting the training into practice is the main focus. Hence implementation and design are centre stage. Needs analysis and evaluation are obviously important and they are covered as well. It is *proposed* that the main responsibility for needs identification putting the training into effect (design and implementation) should fall to the line manager while evaluation should be a joint line/staff effort. Of course, this assumes a line:staff format which may not be evident in smaller organizations, in which case such responsibilities may be encompassed by the line manager or external assistance could be bought in. Assuming some line:staff form, the system must be run on a partnership basis between the executive or 'teeth' arm and the 'support' or staff arm.

If anything, the senior partner ought to be the line manager. In order to persuade the line manager to take back his or her training and development responsibilities, the manager must be comfortable with the theory and practice of the subject, hence this book. The new staff trainer and the experienced manager moving into training from another discipline may find this book useful. Students of training undertaking a course on 'training the trainer' may benefit from dipping into some chapters. More academic students following a human resource course, from the Institute of Personnel Management (IPM) to Diploma in Management Studies (DMS)/Master of Business Administration (MBA), may also find some sustenance from this book.

Objectives

By the end of this text, the reader should be able to:

- Design and develop a training programme.
- Be aware of the management implications of training by using a systems approach to the task.
- Apply principles of learning, particularly to the design/development and implementation phases.
- Carry out a training needs analysis.
- Use the tools and techniques to design and develop a training programme.
- Put into practice specific training initiatives from induction to an off-the-job programme for sales representatives.
- Conduct an evaluation of training.

Framework

The system proposed in the book gives a frame of reference. It allows the reader to come to terms with the concept and application of training. It widens the perspective away from the learner. It does *not* attempt to be a predictive tool, merely a useful checklist for the 'mental map' of the reader.

The proposed system also acts as the framework for this book (see chapter 1). It may be useful to enlarge upon this system.

1 A simple system is used:
INPUTS → TRANSFORMATION PROCESS → OUTPUTS
2 There is a 'feedback loop' from OUTPUTS into the two other processes.
3 The INPUTS concern variables internal to and external to the organization. The main focus is on the perceived need for training and the acceptance of that need within the organization. Such commitment means resources and management time being given to training.
4 These INPUTS are fed into the TRANSFORMATION PROCESS. However, the transformation process is really concerned with developing the training. The learning environment and variables concerned with learning are allied to design principles and approaches to give the overall objectives, content and format of the programme.
5 The OUTPUTS are examined at four levels:
  (a) Induction to skill to knowledge hierarchy.
  (b) Functional or technical expertise.
  (c) Occupational or job expertise.
  (d) Organizational.
6 Lastly, the evaluation process provides feedback to the system.

Indicative Content

The acceptance of the value of training by the organization and its commitment to resources allocated to training is the main subject of the first chapter.

The limitations of training and the range of potential solutions to 'training problems' are noted. The first chapter advocates the professional approach to training using a systems framework. These self-evident advantages of training may not be enough to sustain organizational commitment to training and we return to this marketing/selling approach in the final chapter.

Chapter 2 concerns the 'management' of training: role, function, philosophy and approach. The line:staff interface and the responsibilities for action are discussed.

Learning, the oil of the whole training system, is the 'input' subject of chapter 3. Chapter 4 is linked to the acceptance of training, examining need, from environmental analysis to organizational triggers for training. Various 'how to' approaches are examined in this input category.

Design and development from principles to techniques are then covered in chapter 5 as part of the transformation process. The sixth chapter is about putting the training into place or 'implementing the training programme'.

Four levels of 'intervention' – individual, job, function and organization – conclude the 'outputs' aspect of the training in chapter 7. The final chapter, 8, as is fitting, deals with evaluation and audit as well as maintaining the momentum for training within the organization.

Format

The style and layout of the book needs a brief mention.

- Each chapter has specific learning objectives.
- Endnotes, not footnotes, are used in order to be as unobtrusive as possible and not to disrupt the flow.
- There are many lists, tables, figures and 'boxed' examples and summaries, which provide emphasis and clarity to the text.
- Checklists are given to help the busy manager/reader.
- There is a selected bibliography at the end of the book.
- Cases, often based on reality but camouflaged to protect individuals, are used throughout the book to highlight particular issues.

A Quick Guide to the Book

Issue	*Refer to*
How can I measure the impact of my existing training?	Chapter 8 and 'The Audit' in appendix 8C.
I have a staff performance problem. How do I know it is a training issue?	Chapter 1 and particularly chapter 4 on needs analysis.
What are the benefits of training?	Chapter 1.
How can I 'sell' training to the non-believers?	Chapter 8.
What is my specific role in training? What can I expect from the training department?	Chapter 2. (See box 2.2 for proposed allocation of roles.)

How does management in general relate to training?	Chapter 2 and appendix 2A.
What is the difference between training 'strategy' and 'operation'?	Chapter 2 (box 2.3) and early part of chapter 4.
Can I outline the main knowledge and skill requirements needed by a line or staff trainer?	The whole book is relevant, but in particular chapter 2. Appendix 2B for knowledge, and skills in text (box 2.4 for example). See also flowchart in figure 1.1.
I need to know about the principles of learning in a straightforward manner.	Chapter 3 – appendix 3A for deeper discussion.
Training problems and blockages exist in my organization. How can I overcome them?	Chapter 3.
How can I physically go about doing or managing a training needs analysis?	Chapter 4 – various levels covered.
What methods/approaches can I use to do this needs analysis?	Chapter 4, and appendix 4F in particular.
What factors should I take account of when developing a programme?	Chapter 5, and figure 5.1 for a flowchart.
What design methods are available?	Chapter 5.
How can I determine which method is more appropriate than another?	Chapter 5; table 5.2 proposes some learning type of criteria.
I need to have some knowledge of training aids.	Chapter 5, and in particular appendix 5F.
When should I use on-the-job methods and when should I	Chapter 6.

recommend off-the-job
programmes?

What happens when I am called upon to give a lecture?	Chapter 6; in particular box 6.5.
When should I 'buy in' expert help from outside and what criteria for selection should I use?	Chapter 6.
I have new people starting – where do I find principles of induction training?	Chapter 7.
My organization is conflict-prone. Will training in industrial relations have any impact?	Chapter 7.
The supervisors in my firm seem to be ignored by both shop stewards and more senior managers. Can they be trained to be more effective?	Chapter 7.
'Managing change' is the hallmark of my firm. Can training help at all?	Chapter 7.
Now that training is up and running, how can I effectively maintain and promote it?	Chapter 8 in particular, and a browse through the other seven chapters should help.

Notes

1 Training is seen, at this stage, as work-based learning. Development may involve training but it has a wider time frame and is more futuristic and perhaps less concerned than training with improving immediate performance at a given task. The emphasis here will be on training.
2 Specialization by functional expertise is a common factor in every work organization. Even in the two-person firm, one may deal with accounts, the other with customers, while both continue to conduct their technical roles as plumbers or whatever.

This specialization increases with the bureaucratization of the firm, expert knowledge inputs to solve complex problems and the 'natural' structuring of the firm by functional experts with their own specific range of skills. This complexity can be found with support functions such as operational research (OR), organization and methods (O & M), personnel and training, and the legal department providing an advisory service. In the case of human resource management (HRM) both the line manager in operations management and the staff (or support) training adviser share the same resource – people – unlike the lawyers, who can give objective advice on corporate law without impacting on the line manager's territory or responsibilities.

This staff:line interface is well documented in the literature. For example, see L. A. Allen, 'Improving line and staff relationships', and J. A. Belasco & J. A. Arlutton 'Line and staff conflicts: Some empirical insights'.

3 Without denigrating the role of the learner, the strong individualistic flavour of much of this writing – with its emphasis of self-fulfilment and taking control of one's life – has a very strong humanistic philosophy pervading its approach. The classical example of Carl Rogers (*Freedom to Learn*, and *Freedom to Learn for the 80's*) can be cited, with the subject matter being perceived as relevant to learner's needs, student participation encouraged, self-initiated learning and self-evaluation dominating. The philosophy of the individual, with its self-help message and its onus upon personal initiative, may also find a harmonious chord with organizations who wish to do training on the cheap.

4 See Donnelly, 'The training model: Time for a change?'

1
The Training System

Objectives

- To describe the overall scope of training.
- To distinguish between the 'task' and developmental approaches.
- To relate training to education and development.
- To analyse the benefits of training to various parties.
- To use a training system as a basis for
  (a) understanding training
  (b) as a guide to the text.

I've sat in management seminars for twenty years, listening to managers lecturing each other in the need to develop talent, yet we (the UK) have the worst training in Europe.

John Edmonds[1]
'A tough line on training'

Training: Definition and Scope

Training is a process to change employees' behaviour at work through the application of learning principles. This behavioural change usually has a focus on knowledge or information, skills or activities, and attitudes or belief and value systems.

A succinct definition of the scope of the subject is as follows.

... the systematic development of the attitude, knowledge and skill behaviour pattern required by an individual in order to perform adequately a given task or job.   (Department of Employment, *Glossary of Training Terms.*)

Systematic methods ensure that randomness is reduced and that learning, or behavioural change, occurs in a structured format.[2] Clear objectives, with a programme related to them and some mechanism of evaluating them, follow from this systematic process. From this definition, a range of training emphases may be derived, if not a hierarchy of training outcomes:

1 Simple motor skills which demand little knowledge or the application of knowledge, e.g. stamping documents.
2 More complex skills that require some knowledge base, e.g. starting-up procedures for a particular machine.
3 Even more complex skills which require a non-proceduralized application of knowledge, e.g. developing a training programme.
4 The ability to merge skills and knowledge in highly abstract or conceptual contexts, e.g. designing a new bridge.
5 The fusing of skills, knowledge and attitudes to give enhanced social and interpersonal skills as well as greater self-awareness.

This type of hierarchy will be examined later when we examine the design and development of programmes.

A practical example of a hierarchy of training outcomes to which most of us can relate is seen in box 1.1.

Another interesting feature of this definition is that the focal point is the individual. Perhaps this is indicative of the age of the definition (it dates from the very early 1970s), for nowadays many would see training operating at various levels: individual, job, job family (i.e. a collection of similar types of jobs), group, department and even organization. Clearly the level or 'pitch' of the training effort, or intervention, can differ, but it will be argued later that the individual level of need is the easiest to operate and to evaluate.

The definition touched upon the term 'development'. It is worthwhile examining briefly the interrelationships between training, development and indeed education which is a wider based form of development.

Training is work or task-based and it deals with a short time frame geared to the mastery of specific tasks. Education is broader based and traditionally it has dealt with the 'higher order' knowledge or cognitive aspects of learning over a longer time horizon. In the past, it has tended to be institutional-based and geared to raising standards of reasoning ability and judgement. However, in business/ vocational education in particular, a move towards skills and competencies in Britain (epitomized by Business and Technical Education Council (BTEC) and The Management Charter Initiative)[3]

Box 1.1   Example of a hierarchy of training outcomes

Example   Driving a motor car
Knowledge: Would include such things at the position of the various controls, how to operate them and what happens when you do.
Skills: Would include such things as how to start up the car, how to move off, how to steer it around obstacles, how to change gears, how to reverse, etc. All of these things could be practised at the beginning in a field where there is no danger or inconvenience to other people.
Techniques: Would include the ability to apply all this knowledge and these skills to real life conditions on the open road and in the busy city.
Attitudes: The training course would clearly need to try to develop in the trainees the proper attitudes towards such things as road safety, vehicle maintenance, etc.
Experience: According to the objectives of our training course, it may be necessary for our trainee driver to have experience of driving under special conditions, for example, on very rough mountain roads or even in another country where they drive on the other side of the road. The training officer must arrange the training accordingly.

Source: Adapted from ILO, *Teaching and Training Methods for Management Development.*

---

and the 'flight from knowledge' puts much of this education far nearer the traditional skills-base of training.[4] Similarly the adoption of MBA courses for specific management training initiatives[5] can blur the traditional distinctions between training and business education. In other aspects of education, the distinctions would fit more closely the traditional divergent picture between training and education.

Development, under the traditional vision, falls in the middle between training and education. Development can cover the present role or some grooming for future greatness. A cynical view is that we 'develop managers but train workers'. This may be indicative of the lack of latitude, hence the lack of real development potential, in most non-professional and non-managerial jobs.

However, there is still a case for more of a developmental perspective towards training. The traditional view is that learning, or behavioural change/modification, should continue until 'experienced [however so defined] worker standard' (EWS) is reached. Thereafter 'over-learning' can be quite costly, unnecessary and damaging as trainee frustration may enter the scenario. This of course, assumes more of the same, while a real developmental vision tries to get people to think for themselves and to adapt and adopt. Indeed this self-learning perspective with its humanist philosophy is the polar opposite from the traditional scientific managerial task training which reinforces the task specialization of these post-Taylorites.[6]

The UK IPM has taken on board this wider vision of development and attempts to treat it as a form of continuous learning:

> Continuous development (CD) is not a body of theory, nor a collection of techniques; it is an approach to the management of learning. Continuous development means:
>
> ● learning from real experiences at work
> ● learning throughout working life, not confined to useful but occasional injections of 'training'.
>
> For the individual, CD means lifelong learning with a strong element of self-direction and self management. For the organization, CD means the management of learning on a continuing basis through the promotion of learning as an integral part of work itself.   (IPM statement, *Continuous Development* People and Work.)

To meet the IPM's aspirations, short-term task-based learning would need to be broadened out, and the focus would have to be on how the individual 'learned to learn' between various tasks, so that the principles of learning could be moved into new contexts to solve new problems. This 'portable learning' seems a long way off for most employees. However, such 'portable learning' is more a function of education, not training. Personally I would tend to subscribe to this viewpoint. Even then, the limitations inherent in most people's jobs without a wholesale job redesign package makes the CD a great aspiration rather than a reality for most employees.[7] So more of a developmental perspective with its individual orientation does get away from an over-specialized task approach for the benefit of the organization. This leads us to the wider questions of: who should be gaining from training and, indeed, what are the benefits that we can expect from training?

The Beneficiaries of Training

Most commentators would see the beneficiaries of training as being the individual, the organization and the wider economy of the state itself. The real difference in approach lies between those who emphasize the individual needs being met through training and development and the view that training exists by definition as a benefit to the organization.

Perhaps the benefits to the State seem less debatable. The view presented here is that training primarily must have an organizational *raison d'être*, for without this it can easily degenerate into flights of individual navel gazing which actually damage the image of training. Of course, individual need and motivation are important issues when we examine learning (see chapter 3) and training must take place by committed individuals dealing with trainees who see a benefit to themselves in this process. However, individual benefit cannot be paramount; organizational benefit is the best way of ensuring that organizational commitment is given to training.

The Specific Benefits of Training

What can employees get out of training? Perhaps the question is wider: what can employees get out of work? There is a wealth of socio-psychological research in this latter area[8] but it is beyond the scope of this text. Training is best seen as an incentive to the employee and such an incentive can enhance organizational commitment, team effort, customer relations etc. However, on the 'pure' individual level without encroaching upon an organizational impact, innate incentives can be realized through training. For example, the right skills and knowledge can mean job transferability, job promotion, job enhancement and greater job interest. So there is a material need, potential enhancement and pride in good workmanship in the nature of the task all at stake. In 1966, Bass and Vaughan argued that a Maslow-type[9] of 'self actualization', with its self-fulfilment and personal growth through work, could come through training.[10] One of their main premises is that significant learning occurs when the subject matter has significance to the purposes or aims of the individual. This in turn impacts on how the individual learns with 'threats to self' being minimized and involvement of the learner placed on centre stage. This viewpoint is beginning to come close to the 'quality of working life' debate where individuals escape from the 'psychic prison of work'[11] and become involved in organizations in which members are able to satisfy important personal needs through their experiences in the organization.[12]

Hence, the individual benefits would emphasize the growth in human capacities through the effective use of skills and abilities at work which, in turn, would give greater social relevance to the nature of the job in the community at large.

Enhanced productivity and profitability would be the motivation and spin-off expected by the organization. Training is a form of performance management. An example of uses of training (management) is:

- Changing organization structures
- Dealing with problems of growth
- De-centralization
- Changing technology
- Contingency planning
- Inter-unit knowledge requirements
- Integration of policy and philosophy
- Team building.[13]

The result of training (management) is more efficient use of resources from plant to machinery, less waste and scrap, higher performance levels, better quality goods/services, the maintenance of sound customer and industrial relations and ultimately more profitability.

Other benefits to an organization from training individuals are:

- Learning times are reduced.
- Retention of labour may be enhanced.
- The incidence of absence and accidents may drop.
- Job flexibility can increase.
- Attitudes towards the ethos of the organization can be altered.
- A 'cushion' can be made against the external labour market by developing specialized in-house skills.
- Management training can enhance the internal capacity for decision making and planning etc., which can impact on the very growth, if not survival, of the organization.

Examples of the results of these benefits can be cited by studying British Quality Awards in training, which are given by agencies of

---

Box 1.2 The advantages of training

Gleneagles Hotel
Through intensive training, problems of dissatisfied guests and poor staff morale were overcome. Repeat business increased, complaints were reduced, more guests were served in the restaurant and labour turnover dropped by c. 60 per cent.

Lucas Aerospace – Luton
With efficiency in mind and error minimisation to the fore, a total quality approach geared to customer satisfaction used training where it had virtually not existed to give enhanced quality products. Some $2\frac{1}{2}$ per cent of sales revenue was spent on training.

Source: Adapted from J. Seal and M. McKenna, 'British Quality Awards'.

---

the UK government to organizations demonstrating strong commitment, if not excellence, in training practice and initiatives. (see box 1.2).

The various volumes of *Training in Britain* give a comprehensive picture of what has been happening at national level in training.[14] It may be useful to highlight some of the Training Agency findings before noting the national benefit of training.

- In 1986/87 there were 350 million training days (includes trainees and students in vocational education).
- The cost of this training was about £33 billion.
- Employers sponsored 145 million training days, of which 115 were provided for internally (205 million were supported by government schemes/post compulsory education).
- Less than 50 per cent of employees received training in the year (1986/87).
- Almost 50 per cent of employed adults who had left school with no formal qualifications have had no training since school.
- Small companies are less likely than large ones to train, and the construction and distribution industries fared quite poorly as trainers, while the health sector ranked quite high.

The Training Agency report concluded that training was seen to be beneficial, but evaluating the benefits was not easy as only one in forty employers conducted training evaluation.

The report showed that firms with above-average levels of

training had above-average performance, indicated by, for example, growth, profits and investments. The Training Agency report stopped short of indicating a causal relationship, but others have not. For example, a report commissioned by the National Economic Development Council (NEDO) and the Manpower Services Commission (MSC), and carried out by the Institute of Manpower Studies (IMS), contrasted UK investment in training and human resources with that of Japan, West Germany and the USA.[15]

The report demonstrated that education, training and 'work competence' were the key to the respective economic success of these three competitors. Young people had shorter periods of participation in training and education in the UK with over-specialized career routes and little scope, comparatively, for retraining. A qualifications gap existed in the UK. Engineering training was deficient. Training and education were seen as critical areas of human investment (and not just as costs). The information on education and training in the UK was not under an agency and dissemination was often haphazard and patchy compared to these competitors. Our common sense should lead us to accept that a highly skilled team would produce better results. Fonda confirms that higher skill levels do produce gains in productivity and product quality.[16]

The importance of training to the economic well-being of the country and to its competitive status as a nation has been summed up by John Smith, Leader of the Labour Party:

> ... I have ... recommended a European initiative, a public sector expenditure commitment and a fiscal strategy to make sure that investment, particularly in manufacturing, is increased and maintained at the levels necessary ... but I select training as the matter that needs particular attention. (John Smith – Shadow Budget Speech, 1990.)

At micro level, an early 1990s survey in Hertfordshire showed that most of the respondents (49 in total) said that they were interested in employing only skilled or fully trained people who would need no further training.[17] Here we find a cynical view of engaging the benefits of training without the effort or expense – like having a meal at a good restaurant, provided someone else is picking up the bill.

Hence at macro and micro level, the issue may not be the acceptance of the value or benefits of training for they are generally accepted and can be demonstrated, *but the real sticking point is the commitment of resources to training.*

The *Training in Britain* survey shows us that the employers' net training costs for 1986/87 was some £14.4 billion.[18] When the armed forces, agricultural establishments and companies with fewer than ten employees are added, the bill goes up to some £18 billion. The money involved is insignificant when compared to the GNP (gross national product) and it demonstrates that far more government funding and pressure, rather than the 'voluntarist' tradition of leaving it to responsible employers, may be necessary to stimulate a 'training fund'. This is not to advocate the levy system of the Industrial Training Act of 1964, but some compulsion needs to be placed on employers to encourage training and related business/vocational education and also to inhibit the free-wheelers and the poachers who live off the training of other firms.

Johnson, for example, an IPM Vice President has argued for a tax on training.[19] This seems to be in line with the new statutory framework and compulsory training levy on companies advocated by the UK Labour Party.

So where does this leave the reader? Clearly government policy, stick or carrot, can stimulate training and some form of organizational commitment will follow if money is involved. In the absence of such a policy in the current climate, and even if it went ahead, the manager would still need to justify the need for training, design/develop programmes in line with need and available resources, then implement and evaluate the programmes. Arguably, the discipline of training is the same but the use of resource allocation will differ in these scenarios. Again, management, by definition, is in the land of resource allocation and training is only one of many calls on these resources.[20] Assuming a real training issue exists, the strategies for enlisting and securing internal resources for training (irrespective of the external political climate) will be similar. They include:

- Evaluations based on perceived need.
- Cost benefit analysis, etc.
- Selling the function.
- Marketing the function.
- Manipulating organizational politics.
- High levels of sapiential authority based on sound knowledge/skills of learning, the systems of training, training needs and the limits of

training intervention; and competence in design, delivery and the evaluation of different types of training.

Training knowledge and skills without this organizational commitment will be dissipated and if the resources do exist, good knowledge/skills of training need to be spread throughout management and not monopolized by the training specialist. The first five points are the subject of the final chapter on evaluation and commitment while the last point, the knowledge/skill base and training effectiveness of line managers is covered by the rest of the text.

The role of the line trainer and 'who does what' is developed in the next chapter, which will touch upon the other theme of a wider frame of reference than the current norm in the literature of the learner orientation. This frame of reference not only acts as a guide for managers in their organizational realities, but it gives a structure to the book.

Firstly we need to consider the learner. The self-development perspective is geared to self-help philosophies and it appears to be based on the following premises:

Institutionalized training is expensive and often not relevant to learner needs. Certainly the emphasis on the learner is cheaper than institutionalized learning but if the latter is geared to need the relevance should be self evident.

It fits everyone and the individual takes responsibility for his or her own learning. That is, it is adaptable to the different pace/backgrounds of each learner. It means in essence that the learner takes control of his or her own learning. In itself this is fine provided self-knowledge meets aspiration and ability.

Self-actualization seems to be the real goal. A hedonistic philosophy from the USA seems to permeate the approach.

There is an 'anti-expert' slant. The 'shared experiences' of the group mean that the tutor/trainer becomes a facilitator. It assumes that these shared experiences have relevance and that they have an equal, if not greater merit to proceedings than some expert input.

The student participation in the programme is critical. Again methods/techniques revolving around the learner, and almost ignoring the other influences in the system, can give a distortion on reality. To over-emphasize the learner is to neglect, if not negate, the learning or training system. This over-emphasis on the learner has a smell of a Thatcherite-cum-Smiles self-help vision or the introversion and hedonistic philosophies of a hippy hangover from the 1960s.

Let us be clear though: this book is not setting out to discredit the current orthodoxy of self-development and learner-oriented methods and participative approaches. Clearly, individuals should take some responsibility for their own learning, career aspirations and goals, and self-motivation is an important aspect of the learning theories which will be discussed in chapter 3.

One of the main themes of this book is that the individual learner and the associated participative methods and self-oriented vision must be placed in the context of a total learning system. This idea of a learning system has distinct benefits to the line trainer:

- It acts as a form of integration of the various component parts.
- Relationships (causal and predictive) may arise from this system.
- The main elements are pulled together.
- The potential variables which need to be managed are highlighted.

There are many systems and models of training in use. A proposed system is put forward in this book and it is summarized in the flowchart in Figure 1.1. A brief explanation of the rationale behind the system may be useful.

The core covers a traditional view of 'need – design – implementation – evaluation'. It should not be approached in purely a mechanistic cycle, as the parts are clearly related and dependent with some overlap between them. The context of this core is the learning environment, which includes the learner of course. From a manager's perspective training must be managed. Budgets, policies and resources as well as the requisite skills/knowledge etc. produce a realistic organizational framework. But, of course, training does not exist in a vacuum so the external environment must be considered. The training and learning system in itself does not really produce results, and managers by definition have to be goal-oriented, hence the various outputs which feed back again into the process making it a continuous learning system.

This approach has been adopted in the book and the numbers in brackets next to each classification in the flowchart indicate chapter numbers where that topic will be covered.

Notes

1 John Edmonds, at the time of writing this article, was a prominent UK trade union leader and General Secretary of the General, Municipal, Boilermakers and Allied Trades Union (GMBATU).

Figure 1.1 The training system.

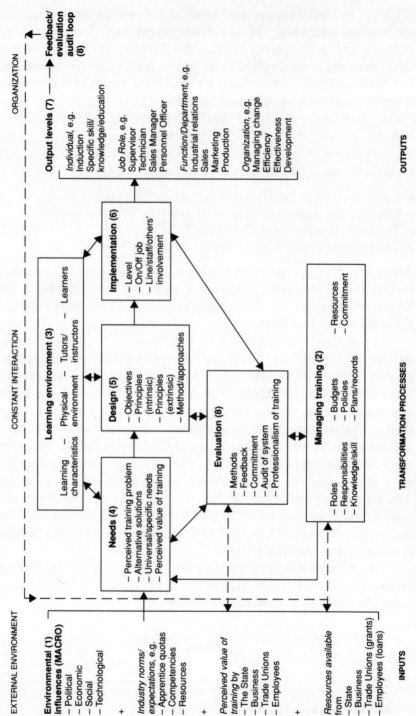

EXTERNAL ENVIRONMENT

CONSTANT INTERACTION

ORGANIZATION

Feedback/
evaluation
audit loop
(8)

Output levels (7) e.g.

Individual, e.g.
– Induction
– Specific skill/
knowledge/education

Job Role, e.g.
– Supervisor
– Technician
– Sales Manager
– Personnel Officer

Function/Department, e.g.
– Industrial relations
– Sales
– Marketing
– Production

Organization, e.g.
– Managing change
– Efficiency
– Effectiveness
– Development

OUTPUTS

Learning environment (3)
– Learning – Physical – Tutors/ – Learners
  characteristics environment instructors

Implementation (6)
– Level
– On/Off job
– Line/staff/others'
  involvement

Design (5)
– Objectives
– Principles
  (intrinsic)
– Principles
  (extrinsic)
– Method/approaches

Needs (4)
– Perceived training problem
– Alternative solutions
– Universal/specific needs
– Perceived value of training

Evaluation (8)
– Methods
– Feedback
– Commitment
– Audit of system
– Professionalism of training

Managing training (2)
– Roles   – Resources
– Responsibilities – Commitment
– Knowledge/skill
– Budgets
– Policies
– Plans/records

TRANSFORMATION PROCESSES

**Environmental (1)
influences (MACRO)**
– Political
– Economic
– Social
– Technological

+

*Industry norms/
expectations,* e.g.
– Apprentice quotas
– Competencies
– Resources

+

*Perceived value of
training by*
– The State
– Business
– Trade Unions
– Employees

+

*Resources available
from*
– State
– Business
– Trade Unions (grants)
– Employees (loans)

INPUTS

Source: Anderson Associates, Personnel and Management Advisors.

2 The mainstream view in training leans towards an experience-based or experiential approach with the trainee being 'exposed' to a range of new situations. Observation, testing, facilitating, trial and experiment, if not error-making, are all part of this doctrine. This book does not wholly reject this viewpoint. It does, however, seek to redress a balance. We need a structure for unstructured learning and the learner is only one part of the equation. Random learning should be discouraged through a structure with parameters for unstructured or experimental learning.

Training can be sub-divided into 'on-the-job' training managed by the line officer or manager; 'off-the-job' training such as a formal seminar conducted by specialists or staff trainers; and vestibule training, which is a half-way house, such as a local technical college training car mechanics with relevant pits and garage tools.

3 BTEC is a council set up to co-ordinate and monitor UK business and technical education.

The Management Charter Initiative is an attempt by leading UK companies to 'professionalize' management education by using core, or uniform, standards of 'competency' at work.

4 This 'flight from knowledge' towards skills is epitomized by the competency and skills acquisition debate in management education. See for example, CNAA, *A Feasibility Study on a National Framework of Assessment Arrangements for Management Education*. Althusser would probably accept that this merging of training and education is a natural and overt example of the socialization of labour by the ruling elite. See Althusser, *Lenin and Philosophy and Other Essays*.

5 Some UK examples include MBAs at City University Business School in London and Middlesex Business School.

6 There is a parallel here between this debate on 'continuous development' with that of 'job redesign'. Both attempt to humanize work to give greater job satisfaction in the face of some post-Taylorite vision of reductionism in the name of efficiency. The work of Taylor and his disciples still seem to be evident in most job design which must inhibit the liberalization of work and development, continuous or otherwise. For scientific management see:

(a) F. W. Taylor, *Scientific Management*.
(b) L. M. Gilbreth, *The Psychology of Management*.
(c) E. A. Locke, 'The Ideas of Frederick W. Taylor: An Evaluation'.

For a refreshing review of managerial approaches to work and labour, and hence development by implication, see G. Palmer, *British Industrial Relations*, chapters 2 and 3.

7 A 'small job' still remains a 'small job' in spite of attempts to enlarge it. If the discretionary aim is not linked to real responsibility and meaning, the job is doomed to stay small.

8 For psychology see, for example, E. E. Lawler and L. W. Porter, 'The effect of performance on job satisfaction', and for a sociological perspective see C. B. Handy, *The Future of Work*.

9 See A. H. Maslow, *Towards a Psychology of Being*.

10 B. M. Bass & J. A. Vaughan, *Training in Industry – The Management of Learning*.

11 This 'psychic prison' has been coined by S. P. Robbins, *Organization Theory: Structure, Design and Application*.

12 The 'quality of working life' debate can be illustrated by such work as J. R. Hackman et al., 'A new strategy for job enrichment' and A. P. Brief & R. J. Aldag, 'Employee reactions to job characteristics'.

13 List adapted from G. Cole, 'Management training in top companies'.

14 Training Agency, *Training in Britain*. This is a survey of employees' training activities in 1986/87.

15 There has been an ongoing national and international debate between Britain, Japan, Germany and the United States linking 'competition and competency'. Suffice to say, Britain comes out rather badly in this quantification of training and competency between the leading industrialized countries. See NEDO/MSC, *Competence and Competition*.

16 See for example, N. Fonda, 'Management development: The missing link in sustained business performance'.

17 Research conducted for the Hertfordshire Training and Enterprise Council (TEC) in 1991 illustrates the point: as Chris Wright, Managing Director (MD) of the TEC, said: 'Companies must brush up their act on training if they are to be ready to meet the challenges that lie ahead'. Quoted in *Business Review*, April 1991.

18 Training Agency, *Training in Britain*.

19 See, for example, R. Johnson, 'The case for a training tax'.

20 Management has a fundamentally economic nature as it involves choices between limited resources and the allocation of resources that could be used elsewhere. Hence a prime concern of management will be to forecast the relative outcomes from any given allocation of resources, including training.

2
Managing Training

Objectives

- To derive the training implications from the main approaches to management.
- To conduct both a functional and role analysis of management, noting the impact on training.
- To distinguish between line roles and staff roles in training.
- To review the main tenets of research into the trainer's job.
- To allocate the trainer roles to the main parties involved in training.
- To conduct a skills analysis of the line trainer's job.

Training Roles
'... there can be no single statement of what the role of a training specialist should be. It is conditioned by a combination of the objective necessities in his firm, subjective and personal elements brought out by the attitudes of managers, and his own conception of his role and personal skills – he and the job help to make each other.'

T. Leduchowicz,
'Trainer role and effectiveness – a review of the literature'

Overview

We have looked at the concept and definition of training. Now we must do the same for management before fusing the two together to make the main theme of the book.

In this chapter various points are being put forward.

- Irrespective of the school of managerial thought being used, there are training *implications*.

- The 'management of people' runs through much of the literature on management.
- If people management is involved, then training, as part of people management, must be involved.
- Managerial responsibilities for training, excluding smaller organizations (under 200 people) tend to rest with a staff training specialist. This is reflected in the literature.
- Here the line manager is seen as crucial to training actually being put into effect, and hence his or her roles and skills should be writ large, and we term the person a line trainer.

A traditional vision of management can be seen as 'effective planning and the regulation of operations'.[1] People were prominent in the definitions of other management gurus[2] with a three-fold analysis of managing the 'business', managing managers and managing workers all under the important constraint of time. Others took a wider environmental view and looked at management as some form of 'agency' of the community.[3] Before examining the mainstream functional approach and its competitor, the role analysis, we need briefly to look at the various managerial schools of thought with their respective implications for training (see table 2.1).

So, irrespective of the organizational or managerial frame of reference adopted by managers, there are implications for training. Indeed this can be further illustrated by examining the mainstream 'functional' approach and the role type of analysis which is a serious rival to the functionalists.

The functional approach emphasizes the *activities* of management. It has a long history[4] and can be summarized as: planning, organizing, commanding, co-ordinating, and controlling.

The militaristic vision of 'commanding' has been liberalized through time to become 'directing and leading'; while co-ordinating has been absorbed into the organizing/planning function and staffing has now been added. The result is shown in table 2.2.

Clearly the staffing or people function is *the* domain where training would come into its own, but the other functions touch upon training as well.

The reality of what managers actually do in effect is seen by others[5] to differ from the functions of management, which are seen as some unrealistic shopping list. A role analysis is used as being more consistent with reality. This role, or pattern of behaviour associated with a position, involves the manager's view of the behaviour as well as the perceived expectations of others. Some ten roles

Table 2.1 Managerial thought and training implications

School	Themes	Training implications
Interpersonal behaviour	Human interaction at work is the focus. Motivation is seen as critical.	Skill development/people management important.
Group behaviour	Workshop attitudes and motivation to act important.	Leadership training. Group dynamics etc.
Co-operative social system	Cohesion encouraged; conflict 'ironed out'.	'Core value' systems and building up a unitary culture part of the brief for attitudinal change via training.
Socio-technical	Constant interaction between social (people) aspects of the organization and technology (equipment/work methods etc.).	Again people part of the equation, so groups/individuals affected by interaction, e.g. new technology/machines etc., hence skill implications.
Decision theory	Organizations seen as a 'complex web of interlocking structures'. Analyse decision – processes.	In many ways, management is decision making, shrewd training people 'switch into' the power structures to gain resources etc.

Table 2.1 (Cont.)

School	Themes	Training implications
Contingency	A horses for courses approach. No one solution as it *depends* on the circumstances.	The uniqueness of the culture and organization must be understood and used by the trainer (staff or line).
Systems	The 'conversion' of external environmental inputs to outputs is the focus of this approach.	The changing environment is a useful focal point for needs analysis and the systems approach may give a useful frame of reference to the trainer.
Classical/scientific management	'Scientific' selection and training of workers. Scientific analysis of time. Market division of labour (planners and workers). Differing responsibilities.	Training with its skill divisions seen to be a main premise of this school.
Behavioural	Groups and individuals important to counter the pure 'task' mentality. 'Contented cows give the best milk.'	People to the fore hence training and *development* important to this school.

Table 2.2   The functions of management and training

Function	Theme(s)	Training implications
Planning	Strategies, policies and programmes.	Important aspects of training and linked to human resource/corporate strategy.
Organizing	Structuring, giving assignments and delegating.	The trainer (line and staff) must structure the work/task load.
Staffing	Personnel.	Key aspect for training.
Directing/leading	Guidance/instructions to subordinates.	The manager/trainer may need training in this difficult area.
Controlling	Monitoring action plans/correcting.	The training plan must be monitored as well.

have been identified, which form a gestalt, or integrated whole, in the manager's job – although one or two roles may predominate in a given situation. (See table 2.3.) So, other than in the figurehead type of role, training implications are evident in most of these roles.

Line and Staff Management

In the classical managerial philosophy a clear division is made between line and staff managers. The line manager or 'teeth' arm, derived from the armed services, is the individual who has the responsibility and the authority to execute policy. An example would be the production manager who is in the direct 'chain of command' from the managing director. The staff manager, on the other hand, is an adviser to the line, the 'support' arm, from accountants to personnel managers and trainers, who provide advice and guidance.

The classical view has a marvellous simplicity to it. However, complications do occur. There may be a training hierarchy as well so that the training director/manager is in effect a line manager to his or her own staff. The line/staff split assumes that authority is

Table 2.3 The roles of management and training implications

Role [a]	Theme	Training implications
Interpersonal		
1 Figurehead	Legal and ceremonial duties.	Training? (social graces?)
2 Liaison	Network of external contacts.	Important information source.
3 Leader	Hires, trains, promotes and dismisses.	Clear training role.
Informational		
4 Monitor	Receiving information (external/internal).	'Control' aspect for policies etc.
5 Disseminator	Gives out information and values.	Training is dissemination of information etc.
6 Spokesman	Giving information to groups (external).	Possible liaison type of trainer role but usually *internal* activity.
Decisional		
7 Entrepreneur	Initiates and designs much of the controlled organizational change.	Clear trainer's role.
8 Disturbance handler	Removing obstacles to change etc.	Perhaps more of an industrial relations role but 'disturbances' may be indicative of a training need.
9 Resource allocator	Schedules own time, authorizes actions etc.	Training competes here for the resources of the manager/organization.
10 Negotiator	Bargaining role.	Very important in getting resources plus convincing subordinates of value etc. of training.

[a] Roles adapted from H. Mintzberg, *The Nature of Managerial Work.*

vested in the job holder by the organization. But authority is also personal and may cut across the line/staff divide. Likewise, control may be horizontal as well as vertical with levels being bypassed by both line and staff managers. However, as in personnel management, *the responsibility for people is shared in training between the staff trainer and the line manager/trainer.*

In many smaller and medium-sized firms (of under 200 employees) there is no specialist training person and the responsibility for training lies with the chief executive officer who delegates training to the line managers, from production/operations to sales. The focus of training, if it exists, tends to be through pure learning by doing or 'by baptism by fire'. Some individuals may be sent on external courses and the local technical college may provide some apprentice and basic office skills education. Training is not well established in these firms, its value questioned and the need is not generally accepted.[6]

On an anecdotal note, when we first started a consultancy business in 1982, we perceived a potential market in this type of firm. Many months later and thousands of pounds poorer, we came to the conclusion that it was almost impossible to enter this market because the potential customer did not perceive the need for systematic training, and the absence of an internal training specialist was probably indicative of their views. So it was easier marketing to the converted, and since that time it has been staff trainers in companies who have bought-in our services. The same can be applied to others: if the manager (line) has been 'educated' in the value of training, the staff trainer's job is not an uphill task.

At the other end of the spectrum is the more sophisticated approach to training often associated with larger organizations. Training specialists seem to multiply by mitosis, with experts found dealing with sales, clerical, technical and managerial/professional training often housed in a former manor house in rustic simplicity away from the line managers. The professional trainer with his or her high level of sapiential authority derived from a thorough understanding of the learning environment is there, in theory, to service the line manager. The reality, of course, is that the busy line manager has a function or operation to carry on and all too often training can be 'delegated' to the staff specialist. Indeed, the line manager may overview training 'on the job' for new starts etc. and nominate people for seminars and courses, but to all intents and purposes, the training specialist has become the senior partner in the relationship. Consequently, remoteness, learning transfer back to the job, and the practicality of some training 'interventions' can be questioned. Above all else, the staff trainer can work only through the line manager and the issue of 'ownership' arises. This is not the usual view of the trainee 'owning' his or her stake in training, which of course is relevant. Rather, it involves the line manager taking some of the responsibility for 'ownership' as well. *For training to be effective, the 'learning contract' must include the learner, the trainer and the line manager.* This is the 'meat' of this book. The line manager has to become more of a trainer, aware of the value of training, its shortcomings and limitations, with some understanding of a system of training, with a working knowledge of learning principles and how they affect training. Above all else, he or she needs a solid understanding of the systematic training cycle with an awareness of his or her involvement in that process. Hence much of the staff trainer's time spent on 'selling' training to the line can be reduced and a more fruitful relationship be developed between the parties.

The Staff Trainer and Training

The literature is dominated by research studies into the role of the effective (staff) trainer. The role of the line manager is relegated to that of a 'client', a monitor of subordinates' performance with an overview of on-the-job training-cum-induction for new members of the team. Above all else, though, the line manager seems to be a 'buyer' of services. This section will look at the traditional view of 'seller' of the services, the staff trainer.

Some consensus seems to occur in what the specialist training person actually does, i.e. the trainer is:

1 consultant/problem solver;
2 designer/learning expert;
3 implementer/instructor/teacher;
4 administrator/manager/arranger of training.

The UK Training Services Agency[7] suggested that there was *not* an ideal model but that there were four main elements to the job:

1 A direct training/instructing role.
2 An organizing/administering role, including needs analysis.

3 A managing element.
4 An advisory service to management.

The work of Rodger et al.[8] covered staff training practitioners in the public and private sectors. Selecting trainees, instruction, the cycle of training and 'client' liaison were the main duties while administration was seen as peripheral – albeit time consuming.

Operator and supervisory training was the subject of the Engineering Industry Training Board's (EITB) study in 1973.[9] A low-status job with limited job functions and mixed calibre of trainers summarized this study. Needs analysis, design and implementation were to the fore in the Bath Study[10] and administration seemed to be problematic, as in Rodger et al.'s research.

Trainer Effectiveness

Pettigrew and Reason[11] departed from the 'job functions' approach and examined the 'best fit' between job role, person and organizational culture. Their study of the chemical industry had a focus in staff trainers from managers, officers to advisers. They identified five 'trainer' types (see box 2.1). These researchers went to great lengths to point out the need for 'congruence' of role, person and culture, to form any vision of trainer effectiveness.

Leduchowicz and Bennett illustrated the 'predominant orientations' of the trainer and his or her job.[12] They isolated two dimensions: (1) 'on what the trainer models his or her activity', and (2) 'how he or she responds to change'. The polar extremes were: a traditional 'educational' orientation and an active 'intervention' of approach; and a maintenance/steady state approach by the change/ dynamic orientation.

From this developed four 'types': the caretaker, the evangelist, the innovator and the educator (see figure 2.1).

They went on to develop this 'congruence' type of approach pulling together the trainer, the organization and their respective joint visions.

To summarize, certain themes are beginning to be established.

• Training roles, without contexts, have been examined. Now these roles can be found in one staff job, as consultant, designer/instructor and administrator. They seem to be less useful for line trainers. The consultant role is not really here, and admin will be taken up with other

Box 2.1 Trainer types and effectiveness

Providers	Maintenance not change; performance-oriented. Likes the concrete and the practical. Nitty-gritty training carried out. Divided into three sub-categories.
	Cultural operator Identifies with mores of organization. Credible but power based legitimacy given to role by organization. May find difficulty in dealing with sub-cultures.
	Individual contributor Good knowledge base, unique personal contribution. Almost charismatic figure. Organizational and bureaucratic constraints may impinge on this individual's 'freedom to operate'.
	Role performer Identified with 'system'. More bureaucratic in approach. Likes paperwork/routine work.
Training managers	Less of a practitioner and more of an overseer. Geared to power and influence. Uses policies/procedures to 'advance' training.
	'Co-ordinators' – Often based at HQ, subordinates may have 'dotted line' relationship. Manipulative skills to the fore in this potentially 'no win' situation.
Change agent	Aspire to altering the 'personality' of the organization. Often seen as 'neutral' outside of the structure of the organization.
Passive providers	Low influence. Many trainers in this category. Waits for 'clients'. Involved in endless details/routine work.
Role in transition	'New vision' of the organization but lacks clear role. Marginalization and legitimacy problems abound. Potential for role conflict.

Source: Adapted from A. M. Pettigrew and P. W. Reason, *Alternative Interpretations of the Training Officer Role*.

Figure 2.1   Trainer effectiveness

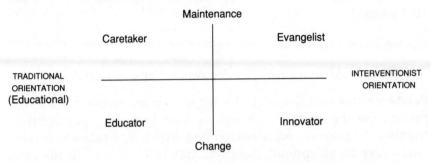

Source: Adapted from T. Leduchowicz and R. Bennett, *What Makes an Effective Trainer?*

non-training aspects of the job. The designer/instructor roles have more relevance and this will be developed later.

- The organizational context is important and roles must be placed in this environment.
- The requirement for competence and professionalism of the trainer (line or staff) almost goes unsaid.
- The possible merging of trainer assumptions and organizational need seems to be the best way of ensuring some 'fit' into the equation.
- The absence of the integration of training and other aspects of the line manager/trainer's job is clearly evident in the research.

Training Roles and Managerial Activities – Integration?

Inherent in much of the research on roles are a range of spectra: passivity to action; reaction to proaction; dealing with structured tasks to ambiguous tasks; and low-level 'maintenance' to high-level problem solving.

It is also felt that there are various philosophies of training, in part emanating from the training department, which for shorthand can be classified as production, sales and marketing orientations. This philosophy is important to grasp as it may constrain the possibility of partnership between line and staff trainers.

Furthermore, if we superimpose the range of managerial functions that we examined earlier we may end up with some integrated approach to management and to training (refer to appendix

2A). From this matrix, an active partnership with a 'marketing' philosophy is seen as a better approach in integrating both line and staff trainers.

Who should do what? Job allocation – line and staff trainers

Before we allocate roles, a brief word is required on other interested parties. On the whole, trade unions have been very neglectful of training. Negotiation for stewards and health and safety representation may be exceptions, alongside apprentice quotas in the craft unions. However, their record on organizational training *per se* is very poor, although some current interest seems to have been generated at last.

Senior management (staff and line) must be involved, external advisers can be a catalyst while the learners' needs must be paramount. A flowchart of responsibility is suggested.

At the risk of being too prescriptive and of ignoring internal cultures within organizations, the following role allocation is suggested: (refer to box 2.2)

Senior management are seen as having a high involvement in policies and evaluating the impact of training. This would involve both senior *line* and *staff* personnel. The latter would have an important 'lobbying' role. As managers, they need to be able to identify needs and help meet training/developmental needs of their immediate managers by allowing transfer to the job. They need to be involved in evaluating the overall 'quality' of training.

Trainees should be involved in the needs analysis and can have coaching/ mentoring roles for other trainees as well as relating learning back to the task in hand. Likewise, they should have an input into the 'quality' assessment.

External advisers should have a high profile in most of the non-administrative tasks.

Unions A low profile is shown as being indicative of their atrocious record in this area.

Training manager/controller If this post exists, the job is the 'linkpin' of the scheme, liaising between senior management and line/staff trainers, trainees and external consultants. Otherwise, the staff training specialist tends to take over this role. If no staff training specialist exists, the line trainer is going to be very busy.

Staff trainer Specialist inputs occur all down the line.

Line trainer This role is highly regarded and shares much of the duties of

Box 2.2 Who should do what in training

Type of role[a]	Trainer roles	Code							
		1	2	3	4	5*	6	7	8
Framework for activities	Training policy formulator	A	A	A	B	B	D	C	C
Goal determination	Training need identifier and diagnostician	B	A	A	B	A	C	A	D
	Generator of ideas for training initiatives	B	A	A	A	A	B	A	C
	Formulator of training objectives	B	B	B	A	A	D	A	D
Preparing initiatives	Researcher and curriculum builder	D	D	B	A	B	D	A	C
	Materials designer and developer	D	D	C	A	A	D	A	C
	Training administrator and organizer	D	D	A	A	B	D	A	D
	Training marketeer	D	A	B	A	A	D	D	D
Implementing initiatives	Instructor	C	C	B	B	B	A	A	D
	Direct trainer	D	D	C	A	A	A	A	D
	Organization Development Agent, catalyst, facilitator	D	A	B	B	B	A	A	D
	Coach, mentor	D	A	A	A	A	A	A	D
	Training adviser, consultant	D	D	A	B	D	A	A	D
	Agent of learning transfer to the job	A	A	A	B	A	C	A	D
Associated activities	Manager of training resources	D	A	A	A	A	D	D	D
	Trainer and developer of trainers	D	D	A	A	A	D	A	D
	Liaison officer	D	C	A	A	A	D	D	A
Evaluation	Assessor of training quality	A	A	A	A	A	A	D	C
	Evaluator of training contribution	A	A	A	A	A	A	A	C

[a] From Leduchowicz and Bennett *What makes an effective trainer?*

Code: 1 = senior line management, 2 = senior staff management, e.g. personnel director, 3 = training manager/controller, 4 = staff trainers, 5 = line trainers/managers, 6 = trainees, 7 = external advisers, 8 = trade unions

Key: A = high level, B = medium level, C = low level, D = nil/virtually nil the staff trainer for his or her unit or department. Again, in the absence of the staff trainer, the line trainer will become a lot busier.

Before we examine the skills required by these staff and line trainers, we need to develop this 'learning partnership' idea between these managers. The staff trainer is the adviser who brings specialist inputs and knowledge to the whole thing. This manager will 'hover' above departmental needs and gives an organizational viewpoint, giving priorities to senior management for their final selection. The line trainers, also line managers in production etc. in their own right, have an important operational input into training. The senior managers (line and staff) have a policy role in training. (See box 2.2.)

The division between strategic and operational duties with demarcation zones for line and staff trainers is evident in box 2.3.

The focus of this book is on the operational activity, particularly from the perspective of the line manager (line trainer). Strategic inputs do occur of course, as in chapter 4, and the staff trainer's role and interface with the line trainer permeates the book. Indeed, reference to appendix 2B gives a 'feel' for typical job schedules of both line and staff trainers.

Skills

Training functions, duties, roles, contexts etc. have been covered. Now we are going to complete this section by looking at the skills required – particularly for the line trainer. Two approaches are used: (1) the traditional knowledge/skills or competency technique, and (2) a taxonomy, or classification, of skills in training. With this knowledge of context, of job role and the skills required, the line manager will be ready to tackle a training needs analysis – perhaps one of the key jobs in the training field that will have to be carried out. But first, skills should be looked at.

Jones, writing in 1983,[13] developed a training intervention skills taxonomy, or classification. It is summarized in box 2.4. This has been written from the perspective of the 'outside' staff trainer 'intervening' in a line department, so we should look for some differences from the perspective of the skills required by a line trainer.

In the *diagnostic* area, the research skills from analysis to design would be very important. The questioning/sensing and communication skills supplement this diagnosis. As the line trainer is 'inside' the department, networking may be less relevant. The ability to get

---

Box 2.3 Proposed strategic and operational roles and responsibilities in training (assuming line/staff format)

Strategic activity	*Responsibility*
Corporate plan	*Senior management with specialist corporate planners'* assistance (unlikely to have training input unless director of personnel lobbying).
Human resource (HR)/manpower plan	*Senior management with HR involvement* at senior level – possibly manpower planner involved – training implications from plan for *all* managers.
Training policy	Statement (action?) of training position. Usually written, or at least signed, by *chief executive*. Should be used as the *'guidelines' for all managers*.
Training plan	Possibly an annual event. Derived from overall policies and corporate/human plans. *Senior training person to draw it up in conjunction with senior line management*. Priorities decided by senior management (line and staff).

Operational activity	*Responsibility*
Needs analysis	Essentially a *line* task as manager has in-depth knowledge of his or her people. Technical back-up and standardization from staff, collated information by staff given to senior management for priority/action.
Design	Traditionally staff role, but learning must percolate through to line. Hence it is proposed that this is a *joint* initiative.
Implementation	Again a *joint* initiative. *Line* manager/trainer has a focus on training 'on the job', and 'off the job' focus given to *staff* trainers.
Evaluation	*Joint* initiative. Shorter time-scale tends to be *line* while organizational view and longer time-scale tends to be staff.

Box 2.4   A training skills taxonomy

Diagnosing   This is research-based and involves both data collection developing constructs/approaches and gaining agreement.

Translating   Understanding the personality of the organization and its ability/willingness to change forms this theme. Converting organizational needs into learning objectives should occur.

Designing   This is the creative phase involving model building and making/learning 'experiences'.

Resourcing   Maintaining a capability to train throughout the organization is involved in this theme.

Implementing Putting training into practice is this main category from workshops to handling 'real relationships' at work.

Enabling   From coaching to counselling, from applying learning to 'influencing' people and events cover this category.

Catalyzing   Making things happen and getting support are these key factors.

Evaluating   Review and results orientation complete the taxonomy.

Source: Adapted from J. A. G. Jones, *Training Intervention Stategies*.

---

a plan off the ground is a typical line management skill which would be used here as well.

The *translation* of organizational need into training need should fit into the business vision of most line trainers. This is not to say that staff trainers are not business people. The individual and group needs can be understood more readily by the line person – provided an objective approach is used. This is a key line trainer area.

Designing 'real' line learning experiences at work can be *the* prerogative of the line trainer.

Resourcing requires money and time as well as political and negotiation skills, particularly with seniors who may control the pursestrings.

Table 2.4 Knowledge/skills required by trainers

Role	*Knowledge*	*Skill*

Direct training	Learning methods
	Technology and aids
	Instructional style
	Skill development
	Information presentation
	Learning objectives
		Deciding learning
		  programme
		Designing learning
		  programme
		Techniques of
		  instruction/
		  managing learning
		Preparing training aids

Organizing	Training systems Resources/requirements	Skills analysis Negotiation/social skills Judging effectively Planning/analysis
Determining	Variety of training needs Costing and evaluating Understanding of own environment	Training needs analysis Problem solving Learning design Social/managerial skills

Consulting	Interactions
	Self knowledge regarding
	  style etc.
	Coaching/counselling
		Interviewing skills
		Testing skills
		Relationship building
		Range of tools of analysis
		  etc.

Source: Roles adapted from Training Services Agency, *An Approach to the Training of Staff with Training Officer Roles.*

Implementation and 'enabling' follows on from design and resourcing availability, but real learning experiences can occur through the line trainer.

Catalysing training is perhaps more of the staff trainer's role, as indeed is *evaluation* where some joint action is necessary to feedback in to the diagnostic area.

The Training Services Agency looked at 'core competences' of specialist (i.e. staff) trainers, and the transferable ones to line trainers (see table 2.4). These aspects will be developed in subsequent chapters.

Appendix 2A Proposed Training Role Spectrum and Managerial Activities

Role spectrum	Passive	Semi passive/active	Active
Philosophy	*'Production'* We have the knowledge/skills. We serve line and they will seek out our assistance if they need it. Reactive – i.e. we will produce if line request it or standardized product range available.	*'Sales'* Still serve line but they may not know our 'product' range. Our role is to go out and convert them to our flag. More of a mission to convert.	*'Marketing'* We are experts but we need 'clients'. We can also learn from the client (i.e. line management). We provide an objectivity and/or a mirror to client needs. Process/facilitating skills and sound relationships to fore.
Managerial implications			
Control	Bureaucratic mechanisms of roles/regulations/procedures to the fore. Control exercised not from within each trainer, but externally by boss and by procedures/roles.	This passes to the 'sales' success and number of converts. Target setting/management by objectives may be used as the mechanism of control. Greater emphasis on individual trainer as well, as trainer needs to control own 'output'/converts. Motivation being emphasized.	They would prefer to emphasize self-control of the 'adviser' rather than externally imposed controls. Project teams/project team leadership gives momentum to the role and acts as a timetable – if not a control mechanism. 'Motivation' preferred to concept of control.
Decision making	Centralized in an authority figure within the training department. Perhaps real decision capability seen to lie outside with line or senior directors (personnel/training).	The focus of decision maker is the 'buyer', but the training department responsible for the design/development/promotion of the product portfolio. Decision making in the training department more decentralized to 'product' specialists, but still retained at the top by authority figure.	They would like to see the decision making process on training as a joint line/staff concept. 'Partnership' with line emphasized. 'Teamwork' within the training department emphasized. Still some vestige of authority at top – but low profile.

Planning	Core product range exists. Hence structured training course programme – by railway timetable. Little adaptability in plan (same as last year). The plan may be top down rather than bottom up.	Important to have a game plan to 'sell' the goods. This may correspond with real needs of clients. Possibility that product range will be packaged – irrespective of plan or need.	Plan may exist. However, danger of obscure developmental initiatives/tangents owing to a facilitating approach. From managerial viewpoint may need more order without destroying creativity of trainers/developers.
Organizing	Job structure may be seen in traditional functional terms with trainers reflecting functions of the organization e.g. sales, admin., technical, craft and management. etc. Jobs may be more 'closed' and duties prescribed.	More fluid job structure to allow selling aspect of job. This will necessitate design/packaging/ promotion in addition to their 'normal' training duties. The traditional functions may be here as in the last category but task boundaries more fluid, thus breaking down the mechanistic aspects of job design.	A matrix or project structure will be evident. This allows some managerial 'control' while encouraging individual specialism and does not destroy creativity. The roles will be more blurred. Possibly called (all) 'consultants' or 'advisers'. More latitude in their work and more 'organic' structure.
Staffing	Jobs are quite rigid in a hierarchy. Performance appraisal may be present. Emphasis on training staff in training methods etc. once recruited. Possibly used as a dustbin for failed and older line managers.	Jobs are more fluid. People with more initiative and 'get up and go' selected into the department. Training in 'product' range/portfolio. Quite keen on new 'product' development. Communication skills emphasized in own training within the department.	The jobs are a lot more fluid. Indeed this can be a problem for management as they may 'do their own thing'. However, may have 'responsible' jobs such as project/ team leader. Select qualified/MBA types. Emphasis on process consultancy (in Schein's[14] terminology); good team playing and working in multidiscipline environment, all noted in training.

Role spectrum	Passive	Semi passive/active	Active
Directing/leading	Formal leadership vested in authority figure of departmental head. Initiatives tend to come from head. Head in turn is given direction by line/senior staff management.	Still leadership/authority figure. Style may reflect need to produce/sell goods. Devolved 'leadership' to trainer who should meet targets. If not met, style may change! Hands on style. Overseeing responsibility/ monitoring.	Still some authority figure but participation is the by-word. Team/ project leaders *think* that they are *the* leaders. 'Hands off' style – more remote. Not a figurehead though.
Communicating	Tends to be vertical and one-sided – from the top. Little feedback from trainers unless individual manager's style encourages 'participation'.	The communication system is geared to the client. The internal system may suffer as a result. 'Honest' attempt at communicating when training department made by manager.	Like decision making seen (perceived = better) as *joint*; that is, between the training manager and the consultants. 'Jointness' may be more apparent than real.

Appendix 2B Job schedules of line and staff trainers

Training Manager Job Schedule

- Assist in formulating training policy.
- Formulate training needs analysis.
- Write training plan indicating priority areas.
- Conduct objective setting.
- Design/develop programme.
- Implement programme with appropriate assistance (department/ one-person firm).
- Prepare training budgets, maintain control.
- Develop/co-ordinate training across organization.
- Recruit, select and train instructors/mentors (staff and line).
- Evaluate effectiveness of training.
- Liaise with external agencies.

Development Adviser Job Schedule

- Develop management development policies/procedures.
- Apply management development policies/procedures.
- Monitor quality of management development policies/procedures.
- Advise on human resource planning.
- Conduct audits of managerial competence.
- Assist in drawing up career development plans.
- Advise on succession planning.
- Develop/maintain an appraisal system.
- Plan internal management development programmes.

Training Officer Job Schedule

- Identify training needs.
- Sell training to manager.
- Gather evaluative evidence on training.
- Select trainers.
- Train trainers/instructors.
- Discuss trainees' progress with line management.
- Plan recruitment (trainees).
- Advise on training.
- Place trainees.
- Cost training.
- Collect statistics.

Line Trainer Job Schedule

- Analyse training needs of subordinates.
- Assist in setting training/learning objectives.
- Inputs/instruction to small groups (at workplace and/or training centre).
- Specialist lecturer/tutor in area of expertise.
- Performance setting and monitoring.
- Conducting – counselling/monitoring/coaching.
- Assisting in planned experience programmes for subordinates.
- Assisting in evaluation of training on the job.
- (Plus other functional duties.)

Notes

1 See for example the then innovative work of W. Brown, *Explorations in Management*.
2 Drucker, for example would see management in these terms. See P. Drucker, *The Effective Executive*. The view of management as a process of 'getting things done through people' has a long tradition.
3 The social responsibility theme versus the purely economic vision is represented in the work of W. G. Frederick, 'Corporate social responsibility in the Regan era and beyond'.
4 This 'managerial activities' or functions approach is epitomized by the early work of Fayol (see, for example, *Industrial and General Administration*). His five 'elements' may have moved on but they appear in different guises (see table 2.5).

   So perhaps in discussing 'management' we need to take account of: control, decision-making, planning, organizing, staffing/directing/leading, and communicating.
5 See H. Mintzberg, 'The managers' job – folklore and fact'.
6 There may not be such a neat correlation between the small size of a company and the lack of acceptance of training, but the author's some ten years' experience of consultancy would certainly bear this out. See also *Business Review*, April 1991.
7 Training Services Agency, *An Approach to the Training of Staff with Training Officer Roles*.
8 A. Rodger, T. Morgan and D. Guest, 'A Study of the Work of Industrial Training Officers'.
9 EITB, 'Training Officers in the Engineering Industry'.
10 See H. E. Frank, 'The Trainer'.
11 A. M. Pettigrew and P. W. Reason, *Alternative Interpretations of the Training Officer Role*.

Table 2.5 Writers following H. Fayol's functions approach to management

Writer	Managerial activities				
Fayol[a]	Plan	Organize	Command	Co-ordinate	Control
Koontz and O'Donnell[b]	√	√	Directing/ staffing	Runs through all functions	√
Stoner and Wankel[c]	√	√	Leading	–	√
Massie[d]	√	√	Directing/ staffing	Communicating	√

and Massie adds decision-making to Fayol's functions

√ = present
[a] H. Fayol, *Industrial and General Administration*.
[b] H. Koontz and C. O'Donnell, *Principles of Management* and *Management*.
[c] J. A. F. Stoner and C. Wankel, *Management*.
[d] J. L. Massie, *Essentials of Management*.

12 T. Leduchowicz and R. Bennett, *What makes an Effective Trainer?*
13 J. A. G. Jones, *Training Intervention Strategies*.
14 E. Schein, 'Increasing organisational effectiveness through better human resources development'.

3
Learning

Objectives

- To understand the concept of learning.
- To discern common learning blockages.
- To develop strategies to overcome these blockages.
- To apply the main learning characteristics to training.
- To relate these characteristics to the main schools of thought.
- To introduce training needs into the learning categories.

A baseness to write fair, and labour'd much
How to forget that learning; *but sir, now*
It did me yeoman's service. Wilt thou know
Th' effect of what I wrote?

William Shakespeare
(*Hamlet*, Act V, Scene II, (34–37))

Overview

Learning, the oil of the machinery of training, is a relatively permanent change in behaviour which is not usually attributable to maturation or growth. Learning requires an 'intervention'[1] by the tutor/manager and the learner in order to modify the learner's behaviour with a view to enhancing performance at work. This 'intervention' can mean the addition of new, the subtraction of old, or the fine-tuning of existing behavioural patterns.

The manager does not have to be a budding psychologist to take learning on board, but the manager does need a good working knowledge of the concepts and the characteristics of learning to carry out effective training. This working understanding can help the manager in the following:

- His or her own self development.
- Designing 'learning events' such as a training course.
- Putting training into practice at that event by delivering the programme.
- Structuring the work experience of subordinates to further new learning on the job.
- Facilitating subordinates' learning on the job through a concerted action plan.

Concepts of Learning

Learning is a form of behavioural modification. In the case of training this change is geared to increasing work performance through the acquisition of modified aspects of knowledge, skills and attitudes. There is not really a body of received knowledge that we can call learning theory. Instead we have differing philosophies and intellectual paradigms.

Examples of this diversity can be quoted. We have a 'rational thinking man' where learning needs to be structured and the 'tell-sell' method is favoured. Memorizing and rote learning would be important responses from the trainee. 'Feeling man' is more fluid, however, with a greater sense of discovery, individual inclination and freer will. The machine-like typology of the rational animal contrasts even more with 'perceptive man' with his self-insight and 'inner mental maps' which reject the crude stimulus-response type of approach of the 'rational man'.

So there is a spectrum from the ultra rational to the ultra emotional with stages in between. Actual behaviour or feelings/ attitudes may be the focal point. From our perspective, actual behaviour that can be evaluated is the most fruitful way forward.[2]

Learning Problems

There are many learning issues which inhibit our behavioural change. Ways of overcoming these difficulties are shown in table 3.1.

Clearly some of these 'pure' learning principles gleaned from the psychologist's laboratory may *not* have an 'applied' transferability to the training environment at work.

Table 3.1 Checklist of learning issues/problems and how to overcome them

Issue[a]	Self	Subordinates	How to overcome
You can't actually come to terms with learning as you don't see it.	☐	☐	You can't see learning but you can't see air either. We *infer* that it has taken place e.g. 'Initial' Stage: X level of performance. 'Learning' occurs: X1 level of performance. 'Terminal' stage: X2 level of performance.
We learn all the time so what's all the fuss about training?	☐	☐	Correct. Without learning we could not leave the cot, so it is ongoing. However, such learning is often non-selective and random. Training is work-led, so it has to have a result and it is usually constructed to remove/minimize 'randomness'.
You can't learn without innate (inner) ability and it's all in the genes anyway.	☐	☐	Some intellectual capacity is required but experience shows that this is under-utilized anyway in many adults. The nature/nurture controversy is a barren debate. Many of our drives e.g. hunger, thirst, sex etc. are bio-chemical/animal instinct, but we have learned/cultured drives as well, e.g. social status etc. So we need both and it's not all in the genes.

Table 3.1 (Cont.)

Issue[a]	Self	Subordinates	How to overcome
The psychologists' learning experiments with animals can't help man.	☐	☐	Man is a *social* animal. However, the scientific experiments were and are, a conscious effort to get away from the subjectivity of the introspection technique/self reporting as a method of investigation.
The laboratory is not the same as the place of work, so there are transferability problems.	☐	☐	Correct. It is the 'pure' versus 'applied' debate. Controls, and scientific rigour would be difficult to simulate outside the lab. Time-scales and evaluation are different outside of the lab. The artificial tasks of the lab do not necessarily meet the 'real' problems of the workplace.

[a] These may apply to your 'mental map' or to your subordinates.

Specific Learning Blockages

Potential difficulties in the transfer of learning principles from the laboratory to the training centre can inhibit if not block learning. Other blockages can be seen as well – these are listed below, together with their effects.[3]

> *Perceptual*　Limited vision of range of learning sources/processes.
> *Cultural*　Individual's background lends itself to planned inputs from specialists.
> *Emotional/motivational*　Any 'threats' to credibility/security avoided.
> *Intellectual*　Learning not seen as ongoing.
> *Expressive*　Communication limitations, hence avoids discussions etc.
> *Environmental climate*　Risk-taking not encouraged by the organization.

The style of the learner, which we will examine in detail later in this chapter, has also been seen as a key blockage factor in learning:

> . . . Some 'blockages' are linked with a manager's learning style. The Activist, for example, looks for action, drama and crisis in a learning situation. Being made to sit and listen or watch is a real 'turn off'. The Reflector looks for time to think: being hustled into a flurry of activity will prevent his learning. If a Theorist questions the intellectual validity of a model, or a Pragmatist doubts the practical competence of someone presented as an 'expert', each will reject the idea or the person and learning will be inhibited. (I. Hinton, 'Learning to manage and managing to learn'.)

The Learning Environment

When we referred to the training system in the first chapter, it emphasized the interrelationships of each part of the system. In this case, learning blockages are not just down to the learner:tutor interface. The learning context, its environment and the organization must be examined. Apart from its overtly humanistic philosophy, the learning variables identified below give a perspective on an *effective* learning environment which removes some of the blockages:

- The potential for curiosity and learning must be encouraged.
- The learning must be relevant to individual needs.

- External 'threats' must be minimized.
- Attempts to change people 'in themselves' is threatening and may be resisted.
- Activity is important for significant learning.
- The learner must take some responsibility for learning.
- Knowledge of 'how to learn' is important to individuals for coping with change.
- Self-initiated learning is longer lasting and all pervasive.
- Self-evaluation can stimulate independence, creativity and self-reliance.
- The trainer/manager's role is that of a facilitator to provide an *environment* in which the learners can set their own goals.[4]

Some of these points are too self-oriented, particularly the last three and are bound by the self fulfilment prophesies of the humanistic approach. However they do give an *aide memoire* for an effective learning environment.

The Learning Organization

Some writers see the organization as a 'learning system'.[5] According to this view, the organization can be seen on three levels which impact on learning:

1 'Theories of action', which inform their actions.
2 'Espoused theories', which they tell the rest of the outside world about.
3 'Theories in Use', which can be inferred from their actions or behaviours.

Hence 'organizational learning' is seen as an adaptive process whereby the 'theory in use' is maintained in some equilibrium with the organization responding to change in the internal and external environments.

However, this concept has limitations. It assumes established norms which become a 'theory in use'. Yet the organization may be a 'multi-goal coalition' rather than some unitarist ideal. Again, is behaviour guided by such theoretical constraints? Is adoption to the various environments more about survival, growth and profitability rather than learning *per se*? Further, can organizations really learn? Is it not the actors in that organization who can or cannot 'learn from experience' etc.? This abstraction of people characteristics to an inanimate organization looks somewhat suspect.

The Training System

The context in which training finds itself does provide both learning opportunities and constraints. Some organizational approaches will be more conducive to training and to learning. If we use the training system in chapter 1, we find the following impact on effective learning and training:

- Organizational acceptance of training.
- Organizational commitment to training.
- The level/degree of resources allocated.
- The value attributed to training.
- The professional approach to training, particularly by the line trainer which reinforces 'value added'.

Hence the system of training is felt to be a broader stage for learning and for understanding blockages and problems in effective learning. We have spent a lot of time on problems and blockages – if they are not understood and overcome, learning and training will not get off the ground. We need to turn to the more positive aspects of the potential 'principles' of effective learning.

Earlier we saw that the concept of learning had diverse philosophical origins which manifested themselves in different approaches. It is very tempting to analyse each approach in depth and come up with common principles. Caution must be exercised as each of these viewpoints have their own territorial integrity, and the weight put upon a 'principle' will differ according to the perspective taken. We cannot have a corner shop 'pick and mix' sweet counter and it is unlikely that an ecliptical approach embracing these diverse schools can be used. So what can we do? We need some guidelines – ones that are positive rather than just guidelines that remove the negatives of the barriers and blocks to learning.

The approach taken is to derive the *main* (it is not claiming to be all embrasive) psychological approaches and then to extrapolate the key aspects of each school. The learning implications are then *derived* from these key aspects. See appendix 3A.

What we end up with is the view that *learning will take place more readily in certain circumstances*. These influences can be manipulated by the line trainer and may exist in the context of the learning or in the specific learning situation itself. So we are going to develop these 'circumstances' and thereafter put some 'weightings' on them according to the *current* mainstream approaches to learning.

The Learning Characteristics – Summary

Motivation   The individual commitment to learn is important and is 'reward' – oriented.

Knowledge of results   This is a form of reinforcement and should stimulate refreshed and renewed activity.

Reward and punishment   The reward, rather than punishment, stimulates and motivates a fresh response.

Trial and error   This is not particularly recommended but it illustrates the experience and the activity of learning. Association and structured repetition is preferable.

Insight   The individual is not a machine and creativity needs room for growth. The individual's 'mental map' is important in this context.

Practice/doing   Action and practice runs through most of these approaches. Again, repetition is important in ongoing learning.

Scale   There is a constant interaction between the individual and his or her environment, so the scope/scale of the subject matter linked to the capacity of the learner needs to be considered.

Individual differences   Individual orientation and relating to 'own' mental map were evident.

Period of learning   This was not to the fore in these studies but it should be noted as another variable for training or applied learning.

Structured repetition   Very important for association and relating x to y.

'Interference'   As this is a communications exercise we need to overcome 'blockages' so this should be noted. Not evident in the various approaches but self evident given earlier 'blocks'.

Transfer   Again not seen as an issue in many of these approaches reflecting the laboratory perhaps, but critical to the line and staff trainers for the carryover of learning to the task in hand. This emphasizes the applied learning of training.

Learning Characteristics – Importance

For the trainer, some of these characteristics are more relevant than others and more 'weight' needs to be given according the main approach. For simplicity, a summary of the three main approaches that seem to be prevalent in the 1990s is:

- Behaviourist/social learning.
- Phenomenological/humanist.
- cognitive/gestalt.[6]

Table 3.2 Learning characteristics related to schools of thought

	Schools of thought		
Learning 'characteristics'	*Behaviourist/ social learning*	*Phenomenological/ humanist*	*Cognitivist/ gestalt*
Motivation – extrinsic	*	*	
– intrinsic		**	
Knowledge of results	**	*	*
Reward/punishment	*	*	*
Trial/error		*	
Discovery/insightful		*	**
Learning by doing/active practice	*	*	**
Scale/part + whole	**	*	**
Individual differences		**	*
Periods of learning		*	
Structured repetition	*		**
'Interference'	*	*	**
Transfer	**	*	**

Characteristic = * Evident, ** Important

This may be at the risk of over-simplification, but there are enough common traits to make these approaches common bedfellows, as shown above. We then relate the learning characteristic to the main school of thought to show its presence and its importance to that school. A discussion of each characteristic follows. Table 3.2 attempts to show the learning characteristic related to the school of thought.

Learning Characteristics – Discussion

Motivation

As we have seen, motivation is related to the level of individual commitment to a task. It is also a critical aspect of learning and can be seen as a form of goal-directed behaviour. However, like learning, *inference* rather than direct observation is the hallmark of examining an individual's motivation. Such motivation goes to the core of the phenomenological approach. It was proposed earlier that the employee should have a goal or goals which training will help to advance. Indeed the individual must be convinced of his or her need for training and of the personal advantages which can emanate from reacting to a fully experienced standard in the job. I have seen this motivational block among experienced managers who come to courses. It is reflected in a range of initial behaviours from apathy to hostility to the common approach of 'I know what management is about and I've been doing it for *x* years'. Again, ask a schoolteacher working among 15/16 year olds designated 'non-academics – no hopes' about motivation and they will reply that their work consists mainly of control not motivation.

Motivation can be divided into two aspects: intrinsic and extrinsic. The latter is outwith the task in hand and may provide an incentive from praise, good relationships, peer-group camaraderie, job security and potential promotion. However this needs to be 'managed' as it may degenerate into pure instrumentalism with the training as a means to a promoted end after successful completion of the programme.

This can be harmful because it destroys the 'safe' learning environment, as people assume that there is some covert assessment of them taking place, and it can mean frustration and disillusionment with training when the expected promotion fails to materialize.

Intrinsic motivation is essentially seen as an 'inner' interest within the task itself. Studying history has always been a personal fascination while, on the personal level, a dental surgeon's waiting-room was preferable to studying physics. The off-the-job/on-the-job trainer must look for ways to stimulate the intrinsic motivation of the trainee. Subject interest and involvement is a two-way process and it does 'rub off' on to the trainee. For example, pride in doing a good job is a useful goal of the trainer and a transfer should be made to the trainee at every possible opportunity.

Hence, wherever possible, the trainer can use attainable incentives to stimulate extrinsic motivation; while the trainer should attempt also to stimulate the longer lasting, more permanent form of intrinsic motivation. Equally, the trainer is not a school master ruling by the cane or tawse: the trainee is ultimately responsible for his or her level of motivation.

Knowledge of results

In line with the social learning theorists, feedback, positive or negative, should allow for some corrective action by the trainee. Again, it can stimulate the motivational process as it acts as a form of reinforcement. We seem to want to know the criterion or criteria whereby we can judge or evaluate our progress and performance. Awaiting essay or exam results is an excellent example of this process.

There may be room for some debate in this area as the rate of learning may increase if the individual is advised of his or her accomplishments. However, if the feedback is too negative and destructive, a demotivational downward spiral may occur with the task being seen as too difficult for the trainee. Hence feedback requires sensitivity.[7]

Reward and punishment

This may sound like a second-rate Russian novel but it is linked to the feedback to the trainee. In crude terms, some form of 'reward' for a desired response serves to stimulate a repetition of that desired behaviour. In line with the humanistic view, this can range from outward praise to 'positive strokes'[8] from the peers as well as from the trainer. At the same time, the 'have a nice day' philosophy of some American training consultancies seems not to strike a chord with many British workers, so care should be exercised in this 'stroking' approach – and it should be genuine.

Punishment may have a place in the military services, police cells and in many regimes throughout the world to curb so-called deviants.[9] It does work, and the brainwashing and beatings of prisoners of the North Koreans and North Vietnamese testify to the success rate. There seems to be little or no place for punishment of trainees in an industrial or commercial environment.

Learning by trial and error

This can be a very expensive and time-consuming approach to learning. It is unsystematic and random. It may work first time, but the individual trainee and trainer has little control over the learning and this approach should not be encouraged. The social learning theorists would stop salivating if this approach were to be encouraged.

Discovery and 'insightful' learning

The stimulus–response–reinforcement model is somewhat crude and may not be too relevant for more complex tasks or for higher level learning objectives, or indeed for more creative or lateral thinking situations. The flash of knowledge, the missing bit of the jigsaw does come to some people but this 'insightful' type of learning requires higher intelligence by the trainee, past experiences which may be relevant, and gestalt type of perception process which sees the situation as a whole, rather than as component parts which are not related. There is a case for insightful learning in judgemental/decision-based learning objectives which will be covered later. The example of de Bono and his approach to creative thinking may stimulate this type of learning.[10]

Discovery learning is not just trial and error either as it is a method of structured or stepped learning which takes the form of an unstructured learning situation. However, the unstructured situation has a context, and 'discovery' aspects, for example in a case study, should come to the fore through discussion between tutor and learner. The phenomenological views and cognitive views are both represented in these approaches.

Learning by doing

If the learner wishes to respond to the initiatives of the trainer, it implies an active rather than a passive role. Any lecturer in a business environment or stage personality (the parallel is not so absurd) can have a nil response from the 'audience' and it can make the task uphill.[11] The aspect of physically doing the task is particularly important for skill acquisition as we would have great difficulty in learning how to drive a car, for example, by only watching the instructor. Of course, demonstration of a skilled performance can help the learner but he or she must perform the task. If it is complex or embarrassing to the learner, or if failure is possible, any risk must be minimized by conducting training in a 'safe' supportive environment. Again, pure repetition of the task or practice may improve performance in most cases.

Scale of learning

Essentially, this can be divided into 'whole' or 'part' learning. If learning a formula for a technical subject, the subject matter would dictate a unit or as a whole. Management techniques of a middle management programme may take some months to input and complexity dictates that the subject matter should be divided into segments or part-learning. Of course, the material and time are not the only criteria, as the intelligence and learning capacity of the trainee needs to be taken into account, alongside the gestalt vision of seeing things as a perceptual whole.

Individual differences

We are all different animals and these different characteristics affect our ability to learn. Motivation has been covered but intelligence needs to be in line with the phenomenological viewpoint and examined as an example of individual differences. Indeed, intelligence is often seen as the speed of response or uptake or the adaption to new concepts. However, industry may not want intellectuals and the slow learner may be as proficient at the task in the long term as the individual who learns rapidly and without effort. Again, there may be some trade-off between intelligence and motivation. As an example, I once worked with a manager of below average intelligence who worked a twelve-hour day almost seven days a week. His long service and loyalty were duly rewarded by the organization and he reached a senior executive position with that low technology company. So motivation *and* intelligence need to be taken into account.

The rate of learning can be affected also by: the tutor; the communication process and the lack of communication breakdowns; the learning environment from the physical setting (try studying next to a building site); to the time of day (after-dinner films are often a snooze session); the peer-group norm; and pressures to succeed, or not to 'bust norms'. The ability of the person to follow directions and instructions and to listen need to be accounted for alongside physical and physiological limits, such as the ability to co-ordinate motor skills in driving a vehicle. Again, some methods that quicken/slow down the pace of learning may be preferred to others by individuals. To a great extent, when the group is of a similar background, for example, first-year graduate trainees, the pace of learning may be more constant but individual differences will still occur.

If this graduate trainee group is given identical inputs, such as 'core competency' aspects of management from planning to controlling, the individual differences would be minimized. Against this, the complexity of the task may make 'uniform' learning quite difficult. Suffice to say individual differences are paramount and need to be accepted as such in the needs analysis, design/development, implementation and evaluation phases.

Periods of learning

Progress in learning seems not to be a steady upward line on the graph. Indeed, there seems to be learning curves. The curve rises steeply at the outset, flattens out, rises and then flattens out. The flat, or plateau, would indicate little or no learning taking place, whereas the upward curve is indicative of progression and learning. The plateau may be seen in cognitive terms of reorganizing thinking and adapting/adopting learning to previous knowledge. Again, plateaux may be indicative of poor instruction, demotivated trainees, inappropriate methods, or the intellectual shortcomings of the trainee.

Structured learning and repetition

The mere repetition of facts does not itself guarantee learning. Learning tables for arithmetic by rote may work, but initial application by a child may be difficult without reciting the whole of the table. Hence, the rote learning may do little for application. However, if it is given a structure whereby the component parts 'belong' together or are perceived to belong to one another, repetition can facilitate learning.

There is some debate as to effectiveness of identical versus varied repetition. Identical repetition means repeating the same few examples or methods over and over; varied repetition may involve using a film or video to give a new slant on the same message. Yet the varied approach is less monotonous (and may impact on the motivation of the trainer and trainee) and a 'varied' approach may strike a different cognitive chord.

'Interference'

A message seems to be more easily accepted and perhaps learned if it does not interfere with earlier learned habits. When speaking to farmers, use agricultural analogies rather than parallels from industrial relations. If the learning can build on prior experience, learning should be enhanced according to a cognitive approach.

Transfer to training

This is related to the prior experience above. If an engineer in a training workshop is shown how to, and allowed to, drill and use the lathe, transfer to drilling and lathe-work on the actual job is facilitated. However, negative transfer can also occur. While undertaking management training, I was fortunate to have an excellent tutor. He had quite radical views on leadership style and he tended to preach on the merits of participation. When junior managers, full of participative fervour, returned to the accounting task they were met by the limiting views of more senior managers who felt that theory X let, alone theory Y[12] was some liberal manifestation which could not be tolerated. To be meaningful, training must be transferable, hence methods, content and format should attempt to simulate organizational reality.

So these learning characteristics should permeate any learning situation. Their respective weights depend upon your approach and views to learning. However, the absence of blockages and the presence of these characteristics in themselves are still not enough to ensure effective training. We need to get below these characteristics to structure specific learning scenarios. Now we are moving into design and development. The distinction is for analytical purity and is artificial in reality as learning characteristics form a key part of the design.

Once the training need has been highlighted, the need must be related to a given learning category. In turn, this category will assist design by linking to learning objectives and to specific design methods. We must turn to learning categories as the last aspect of learning.

Learning Categories

There have been many attempts to classify learning into categories or taxonomies. In themselves these classifications are not too important, but they do have a knock-on consequence to the other phases of the system, design and development, with implications for the implementation phase.

Five categories seem to prevail:

1 'KSA' approach
2 Long's spectrum
3 CRAMP
4 Bloom's taxonomy
5 Gagne's hierarchy.[13]

KSA approach

This is the easiest one to use. It breaks the training need or issue into K (knowledge or information), S (skills or activities), and A (attitudes or belief systems). For example, the industrial relations officer needs a comprehensive knowledge of company policies, procedures, agreements and labour law; skills in communication and interpersonal relationship; and an approachable attitude which facilitates flexibility. Other factors, such as judgement, have been added by some to refine this basic approach. (See discussion in chapter 1.)

Long's spectrum

Learning is classified by Long as a goal spectrum from the tangible goal to the abstract. Skills occur at the more tangible end while interacting with others; a more complex goal occurs at the more abstract end. An oversimplified account is shown in figure 3.1.

So we have a more refined version of the KSA approach coupled to a level of conceptualization along the spectrum of abstraction. The basic skills are easier to acquire than the more refined interpersonal behaviour.

CRAMP

Belbin, in conjunction with Clarke, constructed an algorithm to select specific training methods for training programmes.[14] At this stage, we are more concerned with the different 'classes of learning activity', or the learning classification.

After the training needs analysis is completed, you should ask yourself the following questions:

• Is the aim to develop understanding? If so, this is C (comprehending) type of learning. It involves the understanding and the application of what has been learned in some new way or new set of circumstances. It

Figure 3.1 An outline of Long's spectrum

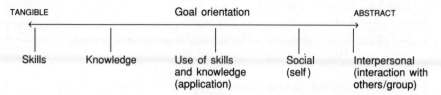

Source: Adapted from C. G. L. Long, 'A theoretical model for method selection'.

must involve positive transfer and as it is not just rote learning, the effects should be reasonably long lasting.

- Is the aim to develop (a) fast reliable responses, and/or (b) manipulation? If so, this is R (reflex) development. These responses are geared to signals or cues. Like comprehension, they are long-lasting but subsumed in a low level of consciousness. That is, it becomes an automatic almost unthinking response.
- If the aim is to modify or develop new attitudes, this is A (attitude) type learning or formation. It revolves around value systems – if not fundamental belief systems. As such, it may be difficult to alter on a permanent basis.
- Is the aim to remember specific facts or figures? If so, this is M (memorizing) learning. The individual may have to recall from memory formulae in a given job.
- Is the aim to acquaint (not to commit to memory) a wide range of easy to follow procedures? In a sense this requires less skill, owing to the simpler character of such procedures, hence P learning.

These are summarized in box 3.1. Very seldom would a learning situation in industry or commerce involve only one of the categories. Several categories may be involved and the trainer must attempt to determine the dominant categories. (Appendix 3B takes this further).

Bloom's taxonomy

Bloom's taxonomy, or classification, while drawing upon an educational rather than training base, usefully embraces the knowledge and attitudinal objectives. The attitudinal aspect is covered by the 'affective domain'. This includes: an awareness and willingness to listen; willingness to react/acquiesce, valuing and sensing worth/commitment; organizing values into a system and determining

---

Box 3.1   CRAMP outlined

C Type – Understanding subject; may be theoretical subject
       – May not have to implement/do anything
       – How, why and when things happen
R Type – Skilled movements involved
       – Will involve practice plus instruction
A Type – Interpersonal relationships to fore
       – Adjustment and acceptance of changes
M Type – Commit to memory given information
       – Action known in a given situation
P Type – Simple/brief
       – No real learning involved, e.g. reference manual

---

value – hierarchies; and finally some characterization and giving a reliable performance of a value system.

The knowledge areas include: pure knowledge or data recall; comprehension or translation/interpretation (which is slightly more advanced than the CRAMP vision of comprehension); application or using a concept in a new context; analysis, or breaking down knowledge into component parts; synthesis, or building up a structure from diverse sources; and finally evaluation, or making judgements about ideas solutions and materials etc. Again there are hierarchies within each domain of both attitude and knowledge. The hierarchies seem to be based on level of complexity. So from a training perspective the application of a concept to a given situation (scenario/case) should be easier for most trainees than a synthesis of the industrial relations system pertaining to the company at that particular time. See appendix 4C for a training example of Bloom's main categories.

Gagné's hierarchy

Hierarchies also exist in an alternative approach by Gagné which embraces both education and training (see figure 3.2). Here we find not only a hierarchy, but a distinct transition between the phases, with mastering an earlier phase being a prerequisite for going onwards and upwards.

Figure 3.2 Gagné's 'hierarchy' of learning

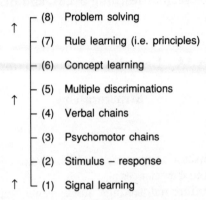

Source: Adapted from R. Gagné, *The Conditions of Learning.*

The hierarchy starts off with basic 'signal learning' and moves on to stimulus/response or association learning. The next two phases seem to be learning lists or chains. Discrimination adds to the increasing aspect of judgement while the sixth level is conceptual. Rules and principles (derived from the sixth level) add to the final, problem solving, level.

It could be argued that the conceptual level or extrapolation from a series of problems should be the highest level. However, this is to split hairs. We find Pavlovian learning and Operant Conditioning, followed by procedural/rule application (see CRAMP) and a judge-mental theme at the top (see Bloom's taxonomy). (See appendix 3A.)

Hence we find some simple learning classifications to fully fledged taxonomies. Some are educational in orientation while others are geared to training. Personally, I find much value in the CRAMP approach and the work of Long is also quite useful for trainers' needs. Both are important when we start to relate learning categories to design and do make the task a little easier.

To conclude this chapter, learning is complex and this complexity has probably been reflected here. However, the complexity must be faced up to, for without a reasonable working knowledge and under-standing of learning, its various conceptual manifestations, and the derived characteristics as well as the learning classification schemes, the line trainer and staff trainer will not be able to make a truly effective contribution to training.

We will consolidate these learning points on design and

development, but first we must go back a step to examine training needs which can be seen as learning needs, and this is the subject of chapter 4.

Appendix 3A   Learning themes and implications

Structuralism

Themes

Emphasis on conscious experiences which create compounds and complexes of structured experiences.
Interplay between internal 'feelings' and external 'sensations'.
'Creative synthesis' in the mind.

Learning implications

Base is immediate experiences impacting upon the individual.
Individual orientation and not machine-like as feelings/emotions are involved.

Functionalism

Themes

There is a purpose or function to life, e.g. survival.
Involves constant adaption to changing environments.
Constant interplay exists between consciousness and experience.

Learning implications

A result orientation is stimulated by having clear purposes.
Learning is not static and is ever-changing according to the purpose related to the wider environment.

Behaviourists (early)

Themes

Associations between items gives some structure to learning, and
the strength of association can show the process between learning and forgetting.

Learning implications

Associations/groupings can stimulate learning.
Repetition increases retention.
Learner transfer can be manipulated.

Classical

Themes

Specific stimulus elicits specific response, e.g. unconditioned stimulus, food, gives an unconditioned response, salivation (Pavlovian Learning).
With conditioning, the salivation (a conditioned response) can be elicited by other stimuli, e.g. bells/buzzers ringing.
Learned stimulus can replace the 'natural' stimulus.

Learning implications

Reinforcement important.
Response can be guided by stimulus.

Operant

Themes

Response preceded the desired stimulus.
Goal-oriented and individual increases response rate.

Learning implications

Reward/punishment
Behavioural shaping/imitation possible.

Sophisticate

Themes

Stimulus/response equation not adequate.
Person responds as well.
'Internalized map' of external environment in animal's brain.

Learning implications

Learning is conscious thought, and through practise it becomes more of an unthinking habit.
Individual differences.
Individual in dynamic environment makes for ongoing learning.

Gestalt

Themes

Holistic (whole) vision.
The whole is greater than the sum of the component parts.
The external world is associated with an internal mental 'map' that allows proximity between the outer and inner worlds.

Learning implications

Learning/problem-solving linked and solutions often seen by reorganizing an holistic view of the environment.
'Whole' learning emphasized.
Relate learning to individual learner's style and 'mental map'.
Case for insightful learning here – not programmed method.
Individual is not just a passive spectator.
Mental map (individualized).

Cognitive

Themes

Animal as a sophisticated type of computer.
Central nervous system as an information system.

Learning implications

Individual differences.
Information oriented.
Capacity to learn and ability to learn will differ.

Social

Themes

Motivation may be related in part to biological needs, but social wants and needs also involved.
Self-actualization and more hedonistic approaches are seen to be near the apex, while more basic drives, e.g. need for water/food/shelter, are seen at lower levels.

Learning implications

Motivation as a key.
Self-help implied.
Insightful/creative approach possible.

Appendix 3B   Task on CRAMP

To conduct a CRAMP analysis from the key tasks of a quality assurance (QA) position.

(C, R, A, M, P) Type of learning

Co-ordinates quality procedures.

Ensures new products adopt effective QA procedures.

Liaises with suppliers and individual businesses to ensure components are the required quality.

Implements production/commissioning test procedures.

Uses statistical methods for faults analysis.

Liaises with customers to satisfy clients on QA.

Inspects systems.

Recommends changes/modifications to systems.

Conclusion. Little P learning here in spite of the procedures, much C given the technical aspect of the job, some R with activities based on systems and some A with supplier/customer contact.

This type of classification is important as it can be linked to the *methods* of training. This will be picked up later.

Appendix 3C   Bloom's Taxonomy

Here are some training examples to illustrate Bloom's training in the cognitive and affective areas.

Cognitive category	Example
Knowledge	Training policy to be known.
Comprehension	Learner to state training need in his or her own words.
Application	The line trainer to use the staff development manual to determine a specific method.
Analysis	The trainer to conduct a needs analysis via a questionnaire.
Synthesis	The manager to write up a needs analysis.
Evaluation	The staff trainer to select the most appropriate external consultant.
Receiving	The line trainer to listen to job difficulties of his or her staff.
Responding	The learner to become positively involved in the group session.
Valuing	Top management to give a written commitment to training.
Organizing	The line and staff trainers to determine the ethics of attitudinal restructuring programmes.
Characterization	The line trainer to be open to the unique situation of each appraisal interview with his or her staff.

Notes

1 Learning has so many definitions depending on the conceptual base and its overriding philosophy. The idea of behavioural change not caused by some physiological process of getting older, or indeed, sicker, is generally accepted as a working definition of the subject.

   The view of 'intervening' is indicative of a conscious effort at learning rather than just letting events occur with some potential for learning which may be realized or may be lost.

2 The process of learning is important but it is felt that in the context of training, the end results or goals are probably more important than the means of getting there, hence the behavioural aspect is emphasized. This issue occurs in Chapter 2 of A. V. Kelly's text on *The Curriculum*, where the objectives of learning are debated in terms of activity and experience versus acquired knowledge and directed goals. This is not to deny the inner value of the learning experience in, say, education, but training needs an outer value in order to justify its existence at the place of work.

3 List adapted from T. Boydell and M. Pedler, *Managing Self Development*. Although the original writers were looking at management, the blocks are applicable to non-managers as well.

4 List adapted from C. Rogers, *Freedom to Learn for the 80's*.

5 For example, C. Argyris and A. Schön, *Organisational Learning: A Theory of Action Perspective*. Max Weber writing on the bureaucratic phenomenon was intrigued at how organizations survived, particularly after the death of a key actor such as the owner. Bureaucracy was his solution, with its office holders, its body of records and a set of received knowledge being handed down. Whilst realizing the concept of bureaucracy has moved on since Weber's time, this 'organizational learning' was in essence the *actors learning* in a very structured and rule-bound organization. See, for example, M. Weber, *Theory of Social and Economic Organisation*.

6 For example, for behaviourist/social learning see J. Dollard and N. E. Miller, *Personality and Psychotherapy: An Analysis on Themes of Learning, Thinking and Culture*, and B. F. Skinner, *Science and Human Behaviour*. See also E. C. Tolman, *Purposive Behaviour in Animals and Men*. For the humanistic vision see, for example, A. H. Maslow, *Towards a Psychology of Being*. The cognitive 'school' can be seen in the work of D. Ausubel, 'Cognitive Structure and Transfer'.

7 The characteristic of 'feedback' has been outlined very well in a case study of the Prudential Assurance Company Ltd. See R. Wood and A. Scott, 'The Gentle Art of Feedback'.

8 The work of Berne is particularly apt in this context of giving 'positive strokes'. He talks of the negative effects of 'emotional deprivation' of the 'stimulus hunger' and 'sensory deprivation'. The concept of 'stroking' implies a recognition and an acceptance of another's presence. A 'stroke' becomes 'a fundamental unit of social action' and an exchange of strokes becomes 'a transaction' which is the base of social intercourse. See E. Berne, *Games People Play: The Psychology of Human Relationships*.

9 Becker's views on deviants is an interesting lesson on learning. Essentially if the individual is labelled a deviant, he or she is seen to be a deviant: and perhaps reinforces the earlier vision or perception and

becomes a deviant. See H. S. Becker, *Outsiders: Studies in the Sociology of Deviance*.

10 See E. de Bono, *Lateral Thinking*.

11 Even experienced comedians 'dry up' in front of 'passive' audiences. See Jasper Carrot's experience as reported by the *Daily Mirror*.

12 Theories 'X' and 'Y' may be indicative of the age of this anecdote from a large British organization, but even if it is dated, so are some of the best vintage wines. See D. McGregor, *The Human Side of Enterprise*.

13 The 'KSA' technique goes back into the sands of time, and 'ownership' is difficult to determine. For the others see later sections on design.

14 See Industrial Training Research Unit, *CRAMP*.

4
Needs

Objectives

- To determine the significance of a training needs analysis.
- To differentiate between training needs and other human resource needs.
- To link training needs to the organizational planning systems.
- To conduct a training needs analysis.
- To select and assess different methods of carrying out the analysis.

If you don't know where you are going, any road will take you there . . .

T. Levitt
'Change and business strategy'

Overview

The 'why' and the 'how' of training needs make up this chapter. The stimulants to training from within and outside the organization are examined under 'triggers for training'. The diagnostic skills of the line and staff trainer provide a focus for this unit while the range of techniques of 'how to do it' are put under the microscope.

The Significance of Training Needs Analysis

Without diagnosis, there can be no solid prognosis. Training needs analysis is the diagnostic part of the whole training process. Failure to conduct a sound analysis means that the whole training initiative, like Napoleon's empire, is built on shifting sands. This analysis is very much concerned with information and data gathering and processing linked to a problem-solving approach of applied research. The relationship between needs analysis is not dissimilar to the affinity between both macro market research and micro market research, and the process of marketing – one feeds into the other and the absence of one makes the subject weaker.

In the earlier analysis of 'who does what on training' it was proposed that the line trainer should have a key role in 'goal determination' which covers the training needs analysis and formulation of overall objectives.

As a way forward we will:

• Define our subject.
• Examine the potential managerial gains from such an analysis and consider the organizational constraints of the real world.
• Highlight the main triggers of training.
• The next part will involve a 'contextual plan of campaign' for the line trainer.
• Lastly, the mechanics of doing a diagnosis will be analysed in depth.

What is a training need? The difference between actual and required human performance at work forms the basis of the need. However, all performance issues are not training issues as the 'substitutability' of resources applies. First of all, it may not be a human performance problem at all. Machines, capital employed, factory space, office utilization, methods of work, etc. can impact on work performance and *may* not have any training implication at all. Likewise, even though it is a human performance problem, the issue may be one of recruitment/selection, incentives or salary/wage administration, welfare, industrial relations, etc., rather than training.

So, is there an 'acid test' for training as the cause? If the problem or issue concerns people's behaviour on some or all of the following categories, it is almost certain to be a training matter: knowledge, skill, attitude, technique and judgement. (See box 4.1)

Advantages

The line trainer has a lot to gain from such an analysis:

• It can be seen if the needs contribute to organizational objectives and if they do not, the exercise should be abandoned as it cannot be justified on welfare/motivational grounds alone.
• An audit can be made of the existing training provision.
• Training acceptance, actual and 'potential blockages' to acceptability can be derived.

Box 4.1   The range of training

Knowledge: Information-based. Should involve some level of under-standing/comprehension. May not involve application. For example, we learn Latin and Greek at school.

Skill: 'Doing' thing or activity. Ranges from simple reflex action, e.g. pushing the red button to stop a machine, to more conceptual skills like writing a book.

Technique: A combination of both knowledge and skill in carrying out a task. It can be proceduralized or relatively straight-forward, such as balancing accounts, or a more complex social interaction, such as selection interviewing.

Attitude: This is more of a belief or frame of reference of indi-viduals and groups. For example as trainers we need to understand the resistance to 'classroom learning' dis-played by many older employees.

Judgement: This is problem solving using the four other categories. Information/knowledge, decision-making skills, the right frame of mind, techniques, probability analysis and the ability to weigh options and derive possible outcomes with an action/decision plan all form the key aspects of this category.

- Sound data is gathered for subsequent programmes.
- Problem identification and priorities can be set as need always outweighs resources.

Constraints

These constraints and priorities need some elaboration. It is un-likely that anyone can have a blank sheet with finite resources to spend on training so realism must be the order of the day.

The commitment of the top management to training, illustrated by the amount of resources made available may provide an organ-izational constraint. The power structure and political reality of the organization epitomized by the ability of the manager doing training to move easily between sections and to move vertically up and down the chain of command, can be a major constraint. A diktat from above may prevail. Hobby-horses from the training department may flourish. Existing courses may develop a life of their own, irrespective of real need. Size, structure, geography, product differentiation etc. may inhibit full-scale analysis.

At operational level, actual costs, resource availability, time, energy, opportunity costs, and priorities as well as the whim of individual managers all impact on the analysis of needs. The role of the line manager *vis à vis* the staff trainer can cause difficulties in 'who does what'. Should the individual trainee have an input into the analysis and, if so, what weighting should this have?

People constraints within the organization are also evident. Time and energy are not finite. Priorities must be made and research purity may have to be sacrificed to commercial expediency. The knowledge of the needs of the analytical methods and skill in applying relevant techniques must be competently understood by the line trainer.

External issues need to be taken into account as well. The degree of training intervention in the organization will be determined by factors ranging from technological change in an industry to government funding for training. Hence much of the 'plan of campaign' and individual techniques linked to level of intervention must be dovetailed into the reality of your organizational life. We could attempt to make a contingency type of approach to training needs analysis,[1] but it is felt that this is too refined and we should attempt to come to terms with a more fundamental analysis of looking at triggers, contexts and nitty-gritty methods.

The Triggers for Training

Useful research was conducted in 1979 which looked at the stimuli for training within the firm.[2] This is summarized in box 4.2. Strictly speaking, these triggers are for general training, but they are indicative of training need as well.

Some very interesting points emerge from this research.

- As we should expect, personnel and training are derived demands within the organization and clearly related to product/service demand.
- Changes in technology and methods of work are a stimulus across the board from small to medium to large firms, with the larger firms seeing them as more important.
- The views of the training department are important, particularly in

---

Box 4.2 'Triggers for training'

The top ten external and internal factors that were seen to trigger training were:

	Overall ranking (sample total 499) (Note: differences occurred due to the size of firm)
External factors	
The anticipated demand for products/services	1st
Forecast profitability (allowing for environment)	5th
Local labour market (existing)	6th
National labour market (existing)	8th
Expected labour market (local)	10th
Internal factors	
Plans to change method/technology etc.	2nd
The views of the line manager	*3rd*
The views of the training department	4th
Recent company profitability	7th
Loss of a key employee (unforeseen)	9th

As an aside, trade union policies, shopfloor views, local educational facilities and government grants trailed in at the bottom of the league table.

Source: Adapted from RBL, 'Research on external and internal influences in training'.

---

larger organizations, while the lower ranking to line may be indicative of the absence of or limited development of professional trainers in these establishments.

- Understandably the small firms are very money conscious with profitability, cash flows and financial forecasts being quite significant. Other important triggers are the fact that the small firm is, of course, more dependent on key employees than is the larger organization, and the state of the local, not national, catchment area of the labour market.
- The medium-sized firms tend to share the main training stimuli with that of the larger firms.

- External factors from training assistance, government funding, local facilities for education and training and 'macro' issues such as education/young people ranked quite low. Clearly training is not seen as a welfare ticket.
- The trade unions from national to local level, trail in at the bottom of the list. Perhaps this is not only because management see training as its prerogative but that the unions in the UK, other than flirting with apprentice training, have not spent much of their initiatives in the direction of training.

A more up-to-date analysis can be derived from the employer attitudes in the Training Agency's 1986/87 survey.[3] When asked 'why train', over 50 per cent of the employers asked stated the need to improve competitiveness. This is keeping with the earlier (RBL) survey but emphasizes the more turbulent external environment of the 1980s. Labour market difficulties in recruiting people were also cited, and customer pressure came to the fore. This is clearly linked to profitability and perhaps to the greater 'quality' awareness of the period. Interestingly, external pressure, funding from the State, health and safety legislation and youth training ranked more highly than in the previous survey. This may be indicative of the initiatives by the State to reduce/redeploy the unemployed in seemingly bogus schemes of youth training in this period, as well as the greater State intervention under the conservative government in legislative curbs on unions and industrial relations during this time. Again, as in the previous research, there is a reactive rather than proactive 'feel' to these stimulants to training.

Clearly, training must be aligned to trading. The training plan must be aligned to the business plan – if both exist.[4] So we must keep this in mind, build a less reactive mechanism for identifying needs and place needs analyses in their organizational context of 'acceptability' as well as promoting a professional approach to the whole subject. We must have a plan of action.

The Plan of Campaign

In large structured organizations, the operational line trainer may be presented with the business-cum-training plan and told to put it into effect. In such circumstances, individual latitude will be constrained but it is unlikely if every contingency has been catered for, so *some* understanding of the context is important for actions to follow the philosophy of the plan. In less bureaucratic firms, more scope for initiatives and inputs into the plan of campaign will be made available to the line operational trainer. So as a *context*, or as a *mode of working*, discussion of the plan is required, covering

- The organization and its environment.
- The organizational objectives.
- The manpower/human resource plan.
- The functional and/or departmental approach.
- The group, job and person level.
- Competency.

Organization and its environment

The actual process of scanning the environment does not really have widespread training implications in itself. Where this successful scanning occurs, it tends to be conducted by top managers and planners.[5] When these environmental scans are moved up to the internal capacity of the organization, to exploit opportunities and minimize threats, human resource issues including training, alongside other resource issues come to the fore.

This organizational/environmental interface is probably best handled by an anonymous case. A major organization based in the UK and involved in information and communication technologies, had in the early 1980s 10,000 employees, 170 offices in eighty countries, and a training staff of some ten people working in cramped offices. By 1990 the training department had grown to some sixty people, only half of whom specialized in technical training. Demand for its commercial services grew and grew, and there were acquisitions in the USA in similar areas of communications. Product changes and a greater sales orientation meant more of a marketing feel and flavour both to the organization and to training. Legislation on unions curbed the power of the journalists, and a change from conflict to relative harmony between management and labour occurred. The economic crash of 1987 impacted on expansion and staff numbers were cut, but the crash also emphasized the need for 'support' services such as training to be in line with the commercial arm of the business: expansion in one meant expansion in the other. In the early 1990s, on technology, the information technology (IT) revolution became all-pervasive in the organization with clear training implications for all job holders.

Box 4.3 Organizational objectives/training implications

Objective	Training implication
Financial/marketing expertise/appreciation	Communication skills. Need for advising employees; seminars on business appreciation etc.
Research/development Product innovation	Unstructured brainstorming. Stimulating lateral thinking.
New technology/acquisition and deployment	Implications for knowledge/usage and for style and approach of management.
Organization structure: mechanism of implementing objectives	Level of decentralization and impact on decision-making capability and style of management. Style awareness/decision making/problem solving.
Ethics	Social responsibility and relationships to labour and community. Sessions for managers/employees debating ethics in business.

Organizational objectives

These are the expectations of the organization which influence survival, profitability, growth and wider social responsibility. These objectives can be 'weighted' into some hierarchy with financial objectives being at the apex of most pyramids. Market position, product development, technology, organizational structure, the view towards employees, and social responsibility tend to be the main features of objectives. There are clear training need implications for each of these objectives, as shown in box 4.3.

An in-depth example is useful. The 1977 Royal Commission on criminal procedure was really the result of pressures, if not wholesale dissatisfaction, with the police objectives concerning community interest in bringing offenders to justice allied to protecting the rights and liberties of individuals.

The UK city riots of 1981 and the Scarman Inquiry[6] showed that the organizational objectives were not being met. Hostility, low levels of trust, communication liaison breakdowns, racial prejudice and harassment linked to a lack of accountability showed that the police seemed not to be meeting their organizational objectives. The Police and Criminal Evidence Act (PACE) 1984 gave a firmer legislation framework for the attainment of better criminal procedures but the critical issue was attitudes and in particular training.

The division was seen as the organizational 'norm' with more individual responsibility and accountability being given to 'line' managers, including staff development and training. The Scarman report had questioned the training standards, emphasizing the need for greater uniformity. Legislative changes and procedure were subsequently given greater emphasis in training. Training has been pushed out to police Divisions and Areas. Competency has creeped into the training programmes for supervision and management training programmes. A core programme of off-the-job and on-the-job training schedules ensures that the objectives of the organization are at least on the agenda, if not being fully met by individuals in the field.

The next levels of the plan will tend to involve more line trainers.

The human resource plan

Manpower has a major influence on the strategic objectives of the organization.[7] Usually, though, it is seen as a 'derived demand' from the organizational objectives.

Again, an anonymous example will demonstrate the relationship between human resource (HR) planning, or the lack of it, and training. Founded in the 1970s the company distributed tapes and records. It had no personnel and training function. Control was concentrated with the owner. On people issues, no HR plan existed, recruitment occurred on an *ad hoc* basis, terms and conditions were not uniform or standardized. Training consisted of a morning on induction and learning with a longer-serving employee. Increased turnover and growth meant increased bureaucratization, and a personnel manager was appointed. Uniformity of conditions, payment scheme reform, record collection and maintenance became the tasks of people management.

Economic recession and the shedding of labour gave way to expansion of profit and labour with new products in the late 1980s. Training remained *ad hoc*. External courses were now being used as *the* basis of any training. No plan existed, no human resource/

business integration existed, there were skills shortages, and lapses in management knowledge, from legislation to coping with people, were a problem.

Bramham provides a useful approach to the whole process of HR planning.[8] Bramham sees manpower planning as concerned with the reconciliation of the demand and supply for labour.

The demand side, with its marketing and financial objectives, can be translated into specific profit targets. In turn, these are converted into human targets taking account of productivity levels, average outputs, custom/practice and efficiency ratios. Hence we can price one hundred (100) widgets at say ten (10) operational people and three (3) support staff at x level of productivity over y time-scale.

The supply side has clear training implications. Labour would be classified by skill/knowledge and job function. Labour stability and wastage can be derived to show the 'flows' through the organization. The resultant internal labour supply is married up to external demand.

Prediction through forecasting for a given period gives a dynamism to the plan. For the line trainer, access to this plan is important. If it does not exist, it is a priority for it has clear advantages for training:

- It relates manpower to business needs.
- A stocktake of existing and future skills/knowledge can be taken.
- Wastage and labour stability are highlighted with recruitment/training implications.
- Skill cover can be derived.
- New methods of work, productivity and efficiency can be noted.
- Training is placed in a dynamic context relevant to organizational need.

Functional/departmental levels

The line trainer will definitely be operating at this level. We must have some framework for analysing the functional or departmental training needs. Argenti, in another context, provides an analytical tool which we can adapt.[9] The main 'functions' are seen as: finance, marketing/sales, research, buying, personnel management and production/operations. Refer to appendix 4A for a checklist covering both organizational and departmental levels.

Group analysis seems to involve several options (see appendix 4B for checklist):

- Job or occupational families used, for example, by the Institute of Manpower Studies.[10] The jobs are linked by common denominators such as knowledge base, and complex job families are created with a shared or similar base. Not only does this emphasize commonality which ostensibly may not be there in the first place, but performance or skill indicators for the group and individuals can then be derived.

● Group dynamics, with its focus on the workings of the group, can be seen as an excellent way of distinguishing between task or objective skills and process or the behavioural categories required to maintain the group and achieve the task.[11]

● Team building is another perspective. A 'model' of an effective team is used and this forms the baseline for the existing team/project/unit to work through their specific needs.

Job level

Perhaps this 'operational analysis' should be job centred. Norms for the job would be established by extrapolating knowledge, skill and attitudinal requirements of the experienced employee (however defined). These norms can be ranked/graded and an importance/ impact to give 'soft' training indicators which can be allied to 'hard' quantifiable targets/outputs of the task.

An example from a marketing job illustrates the point:

Task 'To assess market trends from market analyses, sales statistics and consumer research to identify future product/profit opportunities and potential development of existing portfolio.'
Derived knowledge Nature of market research and specific market; consumer behaviour and buying behaviour/models/approaches.
Derived skill Statistics/numeracy, and practical application of same.
Derived attitude Opportunistic and free thinking.

Although time-consuming, it provides a useful training analysis of the job requirements for the person to measure up to or indeed to highlight the 'training gap'.

Person

(See appendix 4C.) The traditional view has been to focus on the job and skill requirements then, as we have seen, to extrapolate the 'person' aspect. However, the focus has tended to be on skill. For example, jobs were broken down into social/sensory, physical and mental skills. This work was characterized by the link to work measurement and simplification of the task by breaking it down.

These mechanistic visions have been altered by later researchers. For example, the Engineering Industry Training Board (EITB)[12] did considerable work on analysing craft occupations. Initially training needs were analysed from the perspective of physical skills, fault diagnosis and some knowledge. The initial research did not seem to meet the needs of Perkins Engines – it did not meet the balance between general and specialized training. Controls were not established for assessing the level of skill.

A revised analysis was undertaken. It was based on 'total task structure' and 'relations skilled behaviour'. In fairness, other changes also occurred in the revised version including objectives, content, flexibility and measures of effectiveness etc. However, some degree of knowledge seems to be a requisite to the mastery of skill as well as seeing skill as a totality rather than as 'bits' of tasks.

This links to the current debate on job competencies and the individual attaining given national or industry levels (as opposed to organizational criteria which we have been dealing with to date).

Competency

(See appendix 4D.) In the early 1990s, the 'in' theme is competency. It is based on some common understanding and acceptance of a series of knowledge and skills and their application, in given jobs. The acceptability of this concept may be more of a debate in the long term, but it does focus on themes within job categories. It is universal, hence individuality and organizational culture and requirements are shelved. An example of the managerial competency theme illustrates the debate:

I *Managing resources and systems*
   A People.
   B Finance.
   C Systems.
II *Personal effectiveness*
   A Communication/numeracy.
   B People orientation.
   C Results orientation.
   D Self awareness.
III *People* . . . etc.

Competency can be reductionist in its approach. Again it seeks a mediocre norm rather than excellence. Some schemes degenerate into shopping lists of the 'competent person' reminiscent of the 'Great Man' debate in the literature of leadership.

On the positive side, it does give an objective vision of jobs. It works backwards from the previous analysis. It builds the standard, from whatever base, and measures the job/person against this standard rather than building the standard on an organizational basis from the aspects of each job. If the competency theme maintains its momentum, it will mean a rethinking of training needs analysis. Perhaps we will see more organizational competencies arising to reflect organizational reality. If this occurs on a wholesale basis, national norms and levels will fall away and we will be moving back along the track from which we came.

To end this section on levels of intervention, we find that the level of intervention has importance. In a sense, any intervention, if linked to organizational need, has validity. The decision to intervene at a level may well be prescribed for many line trainers. However, the individual job/group levels must be related somewhere along the line to the wider planning horizons of manpower and the organization.

Methods of Determining a Training Need

In practice, the level or pitch of the 'intervention' which has just been covered may determine much of the methods or a given approach to the 'needs analysis'. For example, even in a small firm, there would be little point in conducting a wholesale job or task analysis if the 'pitch' has been at corporate level. Indeed, there is felt to be a strong link between level and method to which we will conclude this section. However, trainers need to be aware of the intrinsic aspects of the range of methods.

Non-specific manifestations of need

A specific needs analysis would not necessarily be the first port of call as there may be problems and issues with associated paperwork, which were not associated with training, from which a training need may be derived. For example, a stream of accidents or flouting of health and safety legislation may point to a problem. Disputes, grievances, high labour turnover or absence levels *may* indicate a manager–subordinate problem, or a manifestation of conflict, or 'withdrawal from work'. The style of management and its approach to people may require further investigation.

Workflow, quality, quantity, output and material waste or scrap *may* indicate some technological, operational or productivity issue linked to training.

Customer, and/or supplier complaints from late delivery to quality of goods or services may also trigger some externally inspired training issue.

As a manager, a sensitivity to these manifestations of problems with potential training implications and solutions is definitely required. Of course, not all such problems are training issues.

Derived training needs from the corporate plan and manpower (human resource management) plan

Plans to grow, merge or reduce operations and personnel will impact on the internal labour supply within the firm. Induction, selection, training, attaining experienced work stardards in a range of jobs, redundancy and counselling will all have implications for training needs at the level of the organization, department and individual job. The corporate plan in action through target setting or management by objectives (MbO) *scheme* will have implications for setting performance levels and getting acceptance from subordinates.

Individual's views of training needs

The individual with some knowledge of the job and organization is well suited to *note* his or her personal training needs. Of course, an 'open philosophy' of management must prevail not to inhibit the individual through some fear of negative and punitive action by management once real needs are identified. This 'do it yourself' element can be seen in some appraisal schemes. Diaries can be a useful method of noting issues and individual approaches to these problems. (See appendix 4E.)

Evaluation of past training needs analysis and training to date

This is often a useful place to start digging – assuming that some training has occurred in the past. Of course, it is historical and may not 'fit' into the current scheme of things. It will give 'clues' to problems and the degree of training put into practice will give an indication (past?) of training, its priority in the organization, and perhaps past training priorities. We need to guard against annual schemes which just tick boxes to demonstrate training need, or worse still, ticking boxes 'for what training course you and your boss think would be helpful' type of approach. This latter approach exists in some very large sophisticated organizations. A lack of past training may give you a blank sheet to work upon, but it may be indicative also of the organization's commitment, or lack of commitment, to training, so beware of making grandiose plans.

The manager's vision of training needs

A sound knowledge of the job and the individual doing the work can make the analysis relatively simple. It may be subjective, though, and anecdotal experience in job evaluation shows that many managers do not really know the real ins and outs of their subordinates' jobs. Observation, sampling of tasks and some form of study of the job/individual interface at work through outcomes or performance may give a more objective stance.

The vision of others

Assessment centres, and psychometric testing as well as simulations in a hotel or training centre may be useful for objective feedback on staff from a qualified third party, particularly where organizational or 'universal competencies' are involved.

Either by using outsiders or by doing it yourself as a manager, writing up an actual case history or event within the workplace, or by highlighting 'critical incidents' at work, may facilitate quick and effective methods of identifying training needs.[13]

Joint or tripartite training approaches

By joint, we are talking about the manager and his or her subordinates and the third party may come from the training department or an external consultancy or agency.

These sessions are geared to training solutions hence some degree of training problem must be evident before you start. Structural interviews with a standardized format give uniformity of treatment while unstructured sessions give more scope for probing and discussion. The repertory grid provides a useful facilitating tool (see later – implementation phase).

For larger groups, or indeed the organization as a whole, questionnaires and tailor-made surveys can be used to gain valuable 'global' information. Sample interviews can be held to back up this method.

Relating level of intervention to specific methods

The more training oriented the approach, the better the quality of information and the better the source for decision making. On this basis, interviews and surveys rank highly. Organizational reality will limit action through resources/energy/effort etc., but some methods are better than others.

On a final point for this section before we go on in chapter 5 to start developing an event or programme, see appendix 4F for a proposed matrix relating method and intervention level which should be self-explanatory.

Appendix 4A   Training needs – primary sources

Assessment of training needs

Survey: (1) organizational level, and (2) departmental level. The principles are essentially the same, but organizational level will be broader, less specific, and more integrated with more 'priorities' shown. You must have one eye on the future and one on today.

Examples of types of information required

Existing situation

Organization	– 'Family tree' with job responsibilities outline for managers/supervisors.
	– Age structure of team.
Products/services/operations	– Materials used/methods of operation and 'processes' of work to highlight technical aspect of various units.
Labour force	– Recruitment trends/shortages of labour/turnover etc. by job category. If possible, length of service of employees by section.
Quality/quantity/output, etc.	– Any problems here? Often trigger training request.
Training	– Assessed in lights of present need(s).
	– Standards of performance required.

Future situation (One to two years only)

- Note changes (environmental and internal to the organization) from product/service to new machinery/procedures, etc.

- Impact on labour force (expansion/contraction/skill mix) by department/ section (knowledge/skill/attitude implications).
- New standards of performance (e.g. quality) to be incorporated.
- Training priorities noted.

Appendix 4B Training needs – primary sources – (group analysis)

Using quality assurance techniques for group problem identification with training implications.

- With the workgroup away from work (e.g. at a seminar), jointly identify problems encountered at work.
- Chair does not have to be section manager, but should have visual aids such as customer complaint surveys, quality control information/ statistics for the group to discuss.
- Free-ranging discussion or brainstorming required with chairperson noting problem areas.
- Zoom into main problems identified through the effect/consequences/ cuts involved: frequency, difficulty, 'preventability', etc.
- Criteria to be ranked in importance to give due weight/rank to given problems and priorities.
- Examine causation, e.g. people, methods, materials, tools, equipment, policies and procedures etc.
- Extrapolate through discussion any 'causes' that are down to knowledge, skill, attitude issues.

Appendix 4C Training needs – primary sources (individual analysis)

Self insight/analysis using the critical incident technique.

Requires:

- Breakdown of the core aspects of the job – however so defined, e.g. knowledge/skills/competency, etc.
- Acceptance by the individual of these characteristics and an agreement on the performance criteria attached to these job roles (perhaps even jointly agreed with management beforehand).
- Some scope for a note on the constraints/opportunities on performance (without degenerating into an 'it's all their fault' syndrome).
- Scope for giving examples of the job performance or looking at 'critical incidents' derived either from the individual, the manager or some joint initiative.

- Taking the context into account and noting what happened during these critical incidents.
- Extrapolation by individual (with guidance from a line/staff trainer) of training and developmental needs.
- An 'open' non-punitive climate where honesty is rewarded. (Critical)

Appendix 4D   Training needs – primary sources

Assessment of training needs (Competency) approach.

- Example of supervisor in production/operations used in a labour intensive area.
- Job 'competencies' derived internally and used as the benchmark to gauge performance and training need.
- Management and supervisor would use this as a basis for discussion on specific training needs and may show differing perspectives on key aspects of the job that need to be ironed out.

Competency	Job aspect	Importance 1 = Low 6 = High	Performance Self/Manager Rank ABCD ABCD
'General management'	Implementing Systems/procedures Reviewing tasks Making decisions Actioning complaints Liaising with other sections	1 ———— 6	ABCD etc.
'People'	Leading and motivating the team Getting co-operation Handling conflicts and negotiating with union Maintaining procedures, e.g. discipline		

Competency	Job aspect	*Importance* *1 = Low* *6 = High*	*Performance* *Self/Manager Rank* *ABCD ABCD*
'Task operation'	Ensuring machinery is at x capacity Output figures reached Waste etc. minimized	etc.	etc.

Appendix 4E   Training needs – some secondary sources

Written material already in existence and not necessarily intended for training.

Views of experts   Often written in a learned journal or in a more popular format.

Good practice   Membership of an employers' association or chamber of commerce may give access to examples of innovation elsewhere.

Health/safety statistics   Trends may be extrapolated to identify a possible training issue, e.g. accidents/fatalities.

Disciplinary records   If similar problems are occuring, it may indicate a lack of understanding by the employees of organizational 'norms' (induction?). It may indicate a heavy-handed managerial style (over-reliance on coercive management) etc.

Grievances/disputes   The stage of settlement being high often indicates the foremen are overloaded. Procedural misunderstandings tend to be rife and negotiation/decision-making skills can be ascertained by scanning these conflicts.

Production/marketing/costing records   Scrap, waste, statistics on usage, customer service complaints etc. can be drawn upon as 'clues' to building up more evidence of real training need.

Corporate/departmental plans   Some trainers don't seem to have access to such documents, but they are invaluable in linking training to the future needs of the enterprise.

Appendix 4F Proposed relationship between method of training needs analysis and level/type of analysis

Level = Organization	Operational (job)						Person (skills)						Individual needs						Core competency					
Job category / Method	A	B	C	D	E	F	A	B	C	D	E	F	A	B	C	D	E	F	A	B	C	D	E	F
Do it yourself	✓	✓	✓	✓	✓	✓																		
Diaries (of jobholders)	✓	✓	✓	✓	✓	✓	✓	✓	✓	✓	✓	✓	✓	✓	✓	✓	✓	✓	✓	✓	✓	✓	✓	✓
Materials/work flows	✓	✓	✓	✓	✓	✓																		
Questionnaire	✓	✓	✓	✓	✓	✓	✓	✓	✓	✓	✓	✓	✓	✓	✓	✓	✓	✓	✓	✓	✓	✓	✓	✓
Formal interviews (structured)	✓	✓	✓	✓	✓	✓	✓	✓	✓	✓	✓	✓	✓	✓	✓	✓	✓	✓	✓	✓	✓	✓	✓	✓
Unstructured interviews	✓	✓	✓	✓	✓	✓	✓	✓	✓	✓	✓	✓	✓	✓	✓	✓	✓	✓	✓	✓	✓	✓	✓	✓
Assessment centre	✓	✓	✓	✓	✓	✓	✓	✓	✓	✓	✓	✓	✓	✓	✓	✓	✓	✓	✓	✓	✓	✓	✓	✓
Appraisal	✓	✓	✓	✓	✓	✓	✓	✓	✓	✓	✓	✓	✓	✓	✓	✓	✓	✓	✓	✓	✓	✓	✓	✓
Self-assessment	✓	✓	✓	✓	✓	✓	✓	✓	✓	✓	✓	✓	✓	✓	✓	✓	✓	✓	✓	✓	✓	✓	✓	✓
Attitude survey	✓	✓	✓	✓	✓	✓	✓	✓	✓	✓	✓	✓	✓	✓	✓	✓	✓	✓	✓	✓	✓	✓	✓	✓
Career plan/meetings	✓	✓	✓	✓	✓	✓							✓	✓	✓	✓	✓	✓	✓	✓	✓	✓	✓	✓
Activity sample	✓	✓	✓	✓	✓	✓	✓	✓	✓															
Reference to experts at the task	✓	✓					✓	✓											✓	✓	✓	✓	✓	✓
Case/narrative account	✓	✓					✓	✓																✓

	A	B	C	D	E	F
Observation						
Audit of personnel data						
Organization survey						
Manpower plan						
Grievances						
MbO/Targets						
Accidents						
New jobholders						
R&D Projects						
Quality control						
Termination interview						
Critical incidents						
Corporate plan						
Group discussion						
Counselling						
Testing						
Evaluation of past training						

Code:

A = Senior Management; B = Other Management; C = Technical; D = Commercial; E = Skilled/Clerical/Manual; F = Unskilled;

√ = Of some relevance.

Source: Anderson Associates, Personnel and Management Advisors.

Notes

1 A contingency approach has been put forward by J. Fairbairns, 'Plugging the gap in training needs analysis'. However, it is a little too 'culture' bound and many other variables must be included to make the thing more viable and realistic.

2 Research Bureau Ltd's (RBL) 'Research on external and internal influences in training'. See also the work of A. M. Pettigrew, P. Sparrow and C. Hendry. 'The forces that trigger training'.

3 Training Agency, *Training in Britain*.

4 The 'Investors in People' programme was launched in October 1991. Very much concerned with linking these two themes of business plan and training plan, it was stimulated by the local TECs. A seminar on this programme by Cambridge TEC (known as Cambstec) in December 1991 was entitled 'Ten good answers to ten pressing questions'.

5 For successful examples of scanning see the *Business Week* article 'Analysis through 1979 and 1980 with the subsequent re-assessment programme'. The companies ranged from Exxon to General Motors. As an example of the involvement of the level/kind of manager in such work, see, J. L. Engledow and R. T. Lenz, 'Whatever happened to environmental analysis?'.

6 L. G. Scarman, *The Scarman Report*.

7 E. Schein, 'Increasing organizational effectiveness through better human resources development'.

8 J. Bramham, *Practical Manpower Planning*.

9 J. Argenti, *Practical Corporate Planning*.

10 Institute of Manpower Studies (University of Sussex). The Institute developed a system of occupational families based on skill, knowledge, know-how, place in hierarchy and educational/professional qualifications. It is known as IMSSOC – The Institute of Manpower Studies System of Occupational Classification. This is a consultancy scheme, and as such it does not appear to be written up.

11 The classical work of R. F. Bales, *Interaction Process Analysis*, epitomizes this behavioural analysis.

12 EITB 'The Analysis and Training of Certain Engineering Occupations'.

13 Personal experience in many organizations has shown this to be a useful and 'safe' entry point. Thereafter, open seminars or open days off the job are held for group sessions chaired by one of our external consultants. Again, confidentiality and 'safety' are important at this initial stage and it is best handled by an 'objective' outsider.

5

Design and Development

Objectives

- To present a coherent approach to learning design.
- To be able to apply this approach in a coherent fashion.
- To be able to distinguish the main methods and techniques open to the designer.
- To select the appropriate technique based on its 'inner merits'.
- To relate techniques to learning objectives and to select the appropriate techniques.

. . . creation disciplines the mind

E. B. White, *The Creative Writer*

Overview

As we have seen, the training system is all interrelated and this design phase very much follows on from:

1 The meeting of a training need.
2 The application of learning principles.

In turn, design and development leads to the implementation stage. Of course, other factors such as resources, policies and managerial roles etc. impact on design and development but are seen as contextual for our immediate design/development purposes.

There are four main themes to this unit:

1 Certain factors are always present in a design and development phase.
2 These principles apply to induction on the job for school leavers to an advanced course at a business school on business strategy for directors.

Figure 5.1   Design and development factors

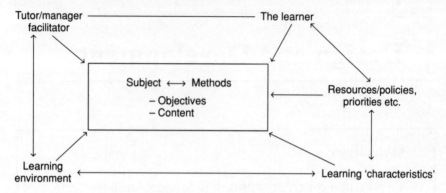

3 The methods and techniques of design/development can be examined 'on their own intrinsic merits'.

4 It is preferable to relate these methods to the objectives being set.

So this creative phase of design constructs a learning situation to meet the training need(s). The mastery of the phase is equally important to the staff and line trainer.

Key Factors in Design and Development

The subject matter, its objectives and content, and the methods or techniques available to put this content into effect, form the core of design. Figure 5.1 shows the main factors impacting on this core. To come to terms with design we need to focus on these factors.

Learning characteristics

The concepts have been covered in a previous chapter, so we will concentrate on the *application* to the design of training.

Learning characteristics and their application to design
Learning characteristic Application
Motivation   The content/methods of the design must be
                                     interesting; boredom and tedium kills off
                                     training. Variety, scope for variation and

	the learner's needs must be evident in any programme.
Knowledge of results	A 'feedback' loop is necessary and must be in-built to any scheme.
Reward	This can be linked to motivation and feedback with finite tasks having stated objectives and time constraints to complete; hence there is a 'reward' or achievement etc. of successful completion.
Trial error	To be avoided.
Discovery insight	Strong case for using this in decision making or comprehensive type of learning situations. It requires a lot of pre-planning by the manager/tutor.
Doing	Activity also stimulates motivation and interest. Some skills must be done rather than 'instructed'.
Scale of learning	The complexity of the subject matter will determine 'whole' or 'part' inputs, with the more complex aspects necessitating more of a piecemeal type of approach.
Individual differences	The pace, style, approach, content, examples and even the methods of design and development will be affected by the 'audience'. Differences in personality, intelligence, perception, beliefs, etc. need to be legislated for – although it would be difficult to meet all such needs in a group programme.
Periods of learning	Breaks (natural and otherwise) need to be thought about – particularly for new entrants who can be overwhelmed in a new environment by the sheer volume of new things to learn.
Structured learning	A sense of belonging and 'hanging together' makes for ease of learning, so common themes/concepts/ideas etc. need to run through the design stage.
Interference	Again a good knowledge of the audience with its own peculiarities can reduce such communications difficulties.

Transfer to work	The closer the design/development is to the everyday reality, the easier is the transfer of learning to 'real' work.

The learner

The individual learner and his or her style seem to be rampant. For design, the background, age, prior learning, educational level and the experience of the learners are all important to getting the right 'pitch' to the design of a programme. Learning events can usefully start with an inventory and discussion on learner style. This allows the trainer to get a feel for the audience and prompts learners to actively think about how they learn. The current emphasis on the learner is indicative of the backlash against 'traditional' learning and of a move to the more trendy participative approach.

The traditional Scottish method of learning in schools (probably replicated in a diluted fashion elsewhere) was based on the following assumptions which have permeated many people's vision of learning: the tutor is the expert; the student is the learner and passive participant; the tutor structures the learning, e.g. home reading and the next session; the evaluation comes through assessments and examinations, set and graded by the expert. To some extent, this is now breaking down with more student participation, on-going assessment, peer-group assessment and group working where experiences (albeit limited) may be shared.

The traditional educational approach would be an immediate turn off for mature adults in a working environment. Their 'hangover' from school/college, may explain some of the resistance that mature people often demonstrate in a training centre – particularly at the initial sessions. Partly as a retreat from this traditional educational model, and more so to put the learner centre stage with responsibility for his or her own learning, if not evaluation, some writers use more of an activity-based *problem solving* approach to learning to characterise the style and approach of the learners.[1]

This problem-solving approach to learning mirrors the everyday method of tackling difficulties as it:

● Generates some guide to 'go on' from your past experience or the use of concepts or principles as your 'map'.
● Modifies or changes the 'map' through experience.

Figure 5.2   Problem-solving approach – the learner

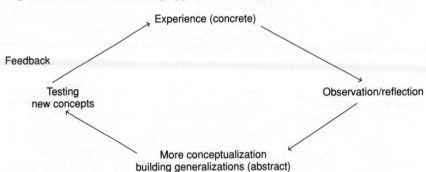

Source: Adapted from D. A. Kolb, 'Towards an applied theory of experiential learning'.

The approach is summarized in Figure 5.2. This approach is *experience led* and assumes that the first port of call is your own past 'life experiences'.[2]

There is an assumption that we go through these phases of learning. To be a well-rounded learner, competency in each of these four phases would be required. Of course, individuals may have preferences within these four stages. Preferences can be seen in appendix 5A.

Honey and Mumford[3] also advocate a learning type of inventory. Again experience, or *experiential* learning, is to the foreground. They seem to go further though: self-knowledge of your learning style is *the* key to understanding and learning from experience. Again we find a 'learning circle' (see Figure 5.3). The four stages are seen to be mutually dependent, although individuals may have a personal bias towards given phases. They then relate these stages to appropriate *learner styles*:

Stage 1 Activist   – 'I'll try anything once'.
Stage 2 Reflector   – 'I'd like time to think about this'.
Stage 3 Theorist   – 'How does this fit with that?'.
Stage 4 Pragmatist – 'How can I apply this in practice?'

The relationship between style and learning situations is explored in appendix 5B. Clearly there is some very useful work in this area. However, if we focus too much on the learner and the learner's

Figure 5.3 Honey and Mumford's learning approach

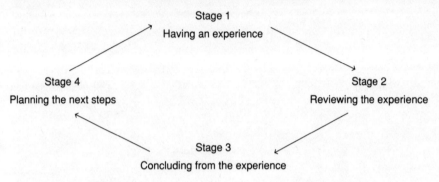

Source: Adapted from P. Honey and A. Mumford, *A Manual of Learning Styles*.

style, the picture will be incomplete. For example, the training system itself is largely ignored; both style classifications assume that learning has a problem-solving orientation (and that may not be the case); conceptualization and the application of (theoretical) principles may be an equally valid experience for learning; and, of course, the learner is dominant at the expense of other more directed or structured inputs. Learning is taken as 'given' but there are many different approaches/philosophies on this subject. Above all else, the self-developmental vision permeates these approaches, and the degree of 'structural/unstructured learning' needs to be added to these style approaches to give that missing dimension.

The work of the style theorists can be developed further by this structural dimension and I use such a checklist in training seminars.

The line and staff trainer

This emphasis on the learner has meant that the tutor, lecturer, facilitator or manager has become the 'support act' in many cases. For design, the level of the trainer's skill, knowledge and ease with particular methods needs careful thought beforehand. Kubr for example, notes the importance of the 'teacher':[4]

> ... to put it bluntly – the teacher (trainer) has to have a clear and significant message to pass, and his personality has to be acceptable to the students or trainees so that effective communication links can be

established quickly and easily ... (M. Kubr, 'Principles for the selection of teaching and training methods'.)

The trainer designing the learning situation must have a mental imagery of the age-group, the experience level, the skill-mix, the educational background and a 'feel' for their general acceptance of training. For example, experienced older workers will expect treatment different from young school leavers. Likewise, the method must be appropriate to the 'culture'. My consultancy experience shows that each organization wants industry-specific material. Cases in engineering, irrespective of the transferability of principles and concepts, do not go down well in a retail environment. Hence care must be exercised in using outsiders unless they are 'tuned-in' to your specific environment.

The learning environment

In general this has been covered, but the designer needs to take account, in particular, of the physical environment. Attempting to explain the workings of a textile machine in a noisy factory can hinder learning; while 'vestibule' training can make learning a much more rewarding experience. For example, gas fitters were trained on the principles at college and in the classroom, then allowed into a simulated workshop before embarking on the outside world. A training environment can simulate a busy sales department before real exposure occurs. The designer needs to be conscious of the physical location of training.

Resources

When times are hard, organizations have to cut costs, and often 'frivolous' areas such as advertising and training suffer disproportionately. In both cases, evaluation of the actual benefits can ensure survival. Even when times are not bad, resourcing training can be problematic. Donnelly, for example, argues that resource allocation/ distribution is one of the most critical aspects of the training system.[5]

The political and business acceptability of training, its perceived benefits, its role in meeting needs, its competition for some resources, and its 'sales' credibility will all impact on resources given to training. We will cover these issues in chapter 8, but it is worth noting this credibility theme, for without it the training is going to be at best limited and at worst inoperative. The attitudes and commitment of top management, budgets and the organizational culture provide clear constraints and opportunities for training.[6] The professionalism of the managers of training goes some way to proving the benefits of training but it still may be an uphill climb.

More 'training type' of issues will impact also on resource allocation, for example:

- How much 'field' work should be given *vis à vis* knowledge based classroom work?
- Do you have selling/or open learning packages of material?
- Can you 'buy in' prepackaged material?
- Can interactive video etc. be used as a tool of implementation?
- When do you time the training? e.g. offpeak times in hotels?
- What is the ratio between on-the-job and off-the-job training?
- Do you need external help?
- What is the priority group to be trained?
- Do you have a training plan derived from the needs analysis to guide you?
- Have you costed out the design/development implications?

Training has no first call on resources. Benefits must outweigh costs and training must be the 'best' solution compared to alternatives if it is to run. These themes are pursued in chapter 8.

These issues must be addressed for training to be viable. Equally, a professional approach by the line and/or staff trainer to setting objectives and designing learning 'events' around these aims can also justify resources for training.

Learning objectives – content

We have a training need and it has been classified under a learning category (see chapter 3). We need more detailed learning objectives standards and performance indicators to keep us on the right road and to help us justify/evaluate training.

There seems to be several ways of tackling the subject of learning objectives:

- Derived from a specific need.
- Extrapolated from some established target or performance management scheme where the criteria are established beforehand for a job.
- Based on a list of competencies or, indeed, sub-competencies or standards, which may be universal for a given job or profession.

Table 5.1　Behavioural objectives: example of a training officer

Action/subject	Criteria	Conditions
After 'training the trainer' he or she will be able to:		
1 Identify the learning styles of the group.	All the group should be covered.	By using a learning style inventory.
2 Classify the learning styles of each individual.	Individuals to be 'graded' according to established classification.	Paper/pencil 'test'. Discussion with each person.

Specific needs　Mager and his 'performance objectives' laid the foundation for analysing learning objectives in 1962 and later, in 1975,[7] he went on to construct a useful method of objective-setting. Learning objectives should contain:

● An action which can be observed.
● Criterion (or criteria) which can be measured.
● The context or the operating conditions under which the performance is occurring.

'Observable actions' should be dealt with first. These tend to be expressed as an action or a verb. For example, 'differentiate', 'select', 'rank', 'provide', 'quote', 'label', 'match', 'repeat' and 'discriminate', etc. These are related to a subject.

The measurable criteria are the qualification of this action. It may be more difficult to achieve in some managerial jobs where the discretionary element of decision making is greater but it should answer the questions: How well? How many? How often? How much? etc.

The 'conditions' are the immediate context in which the person operates and may include opportunities and constraints.

For example, a behavioural/learning objective of a training officer may read as in table 5.1.

Extrapolated from performance management schemes　Probably you will be dealing with some target-setting system, or management by objectives (MbO) or key result areas (KRAs) which can be utilized for training – although this is not their primary function. Take

KRAs for example. It may be useful to go through the KRA system to get a 'feel' for such objective setting. (Refer to appendix 5C.)

Competency and standards   This approach is even more pre-determined as the norms for a job or occupational classification have been established beforehand in some 'objective fashion' and the 'competency' requirement has been laid down.

The *standard* takes it even further as it is more detailed and specifies a degree or level of acceptability. (This 'acceptability' is presumably for management so we need to be aware of who sets the standards.) There would be a list of the acceptable performance criteria (all of which need to be met as they are seen to be essential to the performance). Again there is a context or 'range indicator' showing the 'instances' to which the standard applies. (See appendix 5D.)

To summarize:

- Standards are useful but time-consuming and geared to specific occupations or job classes.
- The KRAs are very helpful at job level but they would have to be in place and then extrapolated for training purposes.
- The learning/behavioural objective is easier, geared to specific learning needs, and facilitates priority setting.

Main Methods Open to the Designer and their 'Inner' Merits

There are many methods available to the designer each with its own peculiar strength and weakness. The list is not exhaustive but we will consider the following:

- Lecture, talk, syndicate/discussion.
- Case, role play, in-tray exercise, business game.
- Project.
- Algorithm, mnemonics, programmed instruction.
- Sensitivity and group training.
- Discovery learning, outdoor training.
- Planned experience, counselling, coaching.

Lecture, talk and discussion

Lecture   This method seems to have survived the ravages of time. The medieval universities to the redbrick colleges have relied heavily on the lecture as an economic way of giving a know-ledge input to many people. It does give a knowledge input into specialized subjects and ideas can be stimulated through a formal lecture.

The modern cult of audience participation and involvement seems to rebel against this method. Some discussion has to be in-built to break away from the 'teacher – student' mentality and the lecturer's style and presentation must take account of the mature audience which typifies training. It is still an economic tool for knowledge inputs if it is handled correctly.

Talk   To overcome the lack of audience participation, feedback, the lecturer, after or during the talk, stimulates some response while retaining the knowledge input in an economic fashion.

Discussion   Good chairing skills, a planned agenda with key quest-ions to keep the momentum are important in this more partici-pative forum. Group size must be optimum and the 'audience' need some basic knowledge/expertise to conduct a meaningful discussion.

Case, role play, in-tray and business game

These methods move away from the 'talk' sessions and rely upon simulating the real world to give practice in a 'safe' learning environment.

Case   A snapshot is taken of a situation and usually written up in an objective fashion with supporting documents from photographs to statistical tables. The aim is to refine the analytical and decision-making skills of the learner. Questions can be in-built or a more open-ended situation given. Film and tapes can supplement the event.

The mini case or incident may be more appropriate for some with a 'happening' occurring without context and the learner has to derive the cause and effect. Altogether the case is a useful problem-solving tool which can link to real cases of the organization. It can be used at various levels of the organization.

Role play   This is the 'movie' of the case-study 'photograph'. By adopting a realistic script, learners are put into situations. Difficulties can exist with people having to assume other identities and acting out scenarios. The roles must be realistic and 'pitched' at the right level: there is little point in asking the supervisor to play the MD.

On the positive side, it allows experimentation and the facility of making errors. The tutor is a facilitator – analytical without being too critical. It can be used for various job roles but the subject matter constrains this method, for you cannot input statistical knowledge via role playing.

In-tray (In-basket) This method simulates the type of incoming work which an administrator, for example, may experience. It aims to further skills of problem-solving, organizing and planning. Time pressures, as in real life, can add another dimension. 'In-file' arrangements of problems, quality and people issues could be used for non-office employees as well. The designer must get the right material for this approach. It should be taxing but not too demanding for a given job role.

Business game This is a sequenced form of group decision making. Usually it covers the main business functions. It can be used for general/senior managers to aspiring young managers. Computer assistance is usually sought. We need to watch that it does not become an arcade game – to be played for its own sake. Personal experience shows this method to be 'fun' for learners.

The project

This can be for technical, operational, administrative or managerial staff. It is an excellent link or bridge between theory and practice. It can be used by individuals or teams. The problem-based approach is useful for creating wider understanding and it can have a functional approach, for example, marketing, or a multi-disciplinary vision. This is looked at again when 'action learning' is discussed in chapter 6.

Algorithm, mnemonics and programmed instruction

Algorithm A true analysis forms the basis of the algorithm. We have seen this when we discussed CRAMP. The 'flow' is usually in one direction with feedback loops for alternatives. A car repair manual, a fault-finding analysis for a technician, and a stock control handbook for a warehouseperson can benefit from this tool. Where answers are prescribed, options are known and ambiguity not tolerated, this is a useful method.

Mnemonics   These are memory aids which can be in-built into programmes. For example, as a student of history and of whisky, the following mnemonic is useful for recalling the post-Napoleonic treaties of peace in Europe: *VAT 69 goes down well with luncheon vouchers.* As I recall, the treaties were *V*ienna, *A*ix la Chapelle, *T*roppeau, *L*aibach and *V*erona. If these were the treaties, the mnemonic works after some twenty-five years!

Programmed learning or instruction   In many ways this approach has been overtaken by open learning and computer-assisted learning. However, it does provide a basis for the self-instruction programmes. The learner works through a series of steps (booklet, manual or interactive video) which lead to well defined goals. Various types occur: 'linear' or straight path is a simple form which progresses step by step, or 'branching' allows more alternatives and greater feedback.

   The schemes are costly, as much capital equipment is normally employed. The method is useful for learning languages and key responses in sales, for example. Clearly, interpersonal skills cannot really benefit from this type of approach and more able learners may become frustrated.

Sensitivity and group training

The polar extreme from the systematic and individualistic approach of self-instructed learning is group dynamics and sensitivity training. The work of Coverdale is a good example.[8] It is based on integrated teamwork. A simple task is allocated but the real emphasis is not on the 'why' of doing it but on the 'how', or the process of attaining the goals. Analysis, decisions, awareness of self and others, group co-operation and conflict, listening skills and leadership can all be stimulated by this approach.

Discovery learning and outdoor training

This growing self awareness is inherent in much of the sensitivity/ group training. Self-discovery is often the keynote. To develop this discovery approach, some unlearning needs to occur and 'taught' inputs must be diluted, if not eradicated. The instructor becomes an initiator-cum-facilitator and the learner takes greater responsibility for his or her own learning. Self-pacing, motivation and greater learner freedom are to the fore. For mature adults who wish to break from a didactic approach, this method is very useful indeed. It does need a denouement, like a plot in a novel being unravelled, so the designer has a lot of pre-planning to do to give a structure to this unstructured learning.

Outdoor training Mountain climbing and orienteering provide a live situation for training people in leadership, group cohesion and interpersonal skills. Participant acceptance, critical for learning transfer, is clearly enhanced by realism and this method can be painfully realistic. One delegate's views on outdoor training were: 'I didn't take our group tasks in the Coverdale programme very seriously . . . but here you've got to because it's for real' (quoted by P. Schofield, 'Outdoor development training').

On the job

Realism is enhanced through on-the-job methods. The learning situation may be less structured at the coalface of the operation compared to the training centre or the interactive video.

'Sitting by Nellie' is a time-honoured approach, where a trainee learns from a more experienced employee. If Nellie is able and can 'instruct' it is better than nothing, but even then the trainee picks up some bad habits from Nellie. For example, try learning to drive from a friend, not an instructor, who has been driving for some years. 'Baptism under fire' is an appropriate term for this approach. Trial by error is costly and can damage the organization's budget and the individual's self esteem.

We need 'planned experience' with learning objectives and learning principles being applied as an off-the-job training and this is a key task of the line trainer. Laird provides a useful summary of three main types of on-the-job training with the emphasis on experience.[9] These are shown in box 5.1.

Coaching, counselling and mentoring are key aspects of developing experience on the job. Above all else, though, existing work processes, procedures and structures such as committees, must be used as the basis for a learning situation which is rigorously planned by the line trainer and which meets the objective criteria normally

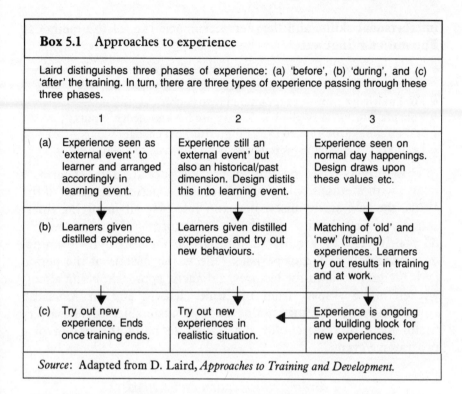

Box 5.1 Approaches to experience

Laird distinguishes three phases of experience: (a) 'before', (b) 'during', and (c) 'after' the training. In turn, there are three types of experience passing through these three phases.

	1	2	3
(a)	Experience seen as 'external event' to learner and arranged accordingly in learning event.	Experience still an 'external event' but also an historical/past dimension. Design distils this into learning event.	Experience seen on normal day happenings. Design draws upon these values etc.
(b)	Learners given distilled experience.	Learners given distilled experience and try out new behaviours.	Matching of 'old' and 'new' (training) experiences. Learners try out results in training and at work.
(c)	Try out new experience. Ends once training ends.	Try out new experiences in realistic situation.	Experience is ongoing and building block for new experiences.

Source: Adapted from D. Laird, *Approaches to Training and Development.*

associated with the job training. These views will be developed under 'implementation strategies' in chapter 6.

Method Selection: Criteria

We have scanned *some* of the main methods and teased out their respective merits on their own terms. Now we are going to apply external criteria to assist us in selecting a particular format.

Objectives and methods

Clearly there has to be a link between the objectives being set and the methods being used. Indeed, methods can be seen as 'objectives in action'. The work of Carroll and others provides us with a useful fusing of objectives and methods.[10]

The researchers looked at various learning objectives: knowledge (acquisition and retention), attitudes, problem, solving, interpersonal skills, and 'learner acceptance' (i.e. of the methods). The main findings were:

- Across the board, case studies, discussions and business games were seen as the most effective methods of meeting all the objectives.
- For knowledge inputs, programmed instruction was useful.
- Role playing was very good excluding use for knowledge inputs.
- 'T' (training) groups were useful for attitudinal change.
- Lectures, TV and films were lower down the scale of 'usefulness'.

This work is based on the 'expert' views of trainers. It forms a matrix with methods/objectives. From this American research of the 1970s, the case study, discussion and role play all involving inter-action and participation do very well. Lectures – TV or otherwise – do poorly. The 'T group' (training group for sensitivity training) does extremely well and perhaps reflects the flavour of the period and this may account for lectures, a didactic approach, being almost written off. So, apart from the time element and an American cultural aspect which may not be wholly transferable, we have a very useful piece of research for the trainer to build the design of a programme/event.

Learning classification and methods

The CRAMP algorithm gives a learning typology and relates learn-ing to specific design methods (refer to appendix 5E). For example, take 'C' or comprehension learning. If we follow the algorithm, we find text books and lectures dominated by this type of learning. When the trainees are more experienced and accustomed to this type of learning, 'discovery' methods can be usefully utilized. This can be followed on for each learning category.

There seems to be *some* limited crossover between Carroll's work and CRAMP, but the objectives differ in concept and application, so a comparative analysis would not be helpful.

Learning objectives, participant involvement and design methods The hierarchy of Long's learning objectives has been discussed (see chapter 3). Allied to these objectives is the degree of trainee partici-pation or involvement. From these two points, Long suggests various design methods. This is linked to Carroll's 'participant acceptance' and to the motivation of the trainee. See figure 5.4. This is a useful approach although the feedback/level of participation is only *one* aspect of the motivational mix of the learning characteristics.

Figure 5.4 Objectives/participation/design

Source: Adapted from C. G. L. Long, 'A theoretical model for method selection'.

'Qualities' and design methods Visions of 'what constitutes an effective manager' seem to be a popular aspect of training. One such approach highlighted a range of qualities which is seen to be associated with 'effectiveness' and links them up to self-developmental methods of design.[11] Burgoyne et al. note that effective, goal directed, qualities of managers have been linked to various design methods. For example:

- *People/social skills* are linked to group working, action learning, structured exercises, development sessions, coaching and counselling and meditation as well as outward bound sessions.
- *Creativity* covered the same design methods.
- *Sensitivity to events*, covered by the same design methods with the addition of on-the-job activities.
- *Basic facts*, include action learning, development sessions, academic education and on-the-job activities, were seen as useful methods for getting to terms with basic information about the job and organization.

Action learning, joint developmental activities, coaching/counselling and outward bound seem to cover most of these 'qualities', but the group is restricted to management and the concept of 'qualities' of effectiveness, whatever that means, can be debated at length. However, some useful themes not dissimilar to the other findings emerge particularly in action learning and outward bound, which I rank highly on their 'inner merits'.

Learning Characteristics, Objectives and Methods of Design

We have examined a range of design methods and earlier we looked at learning characteristics, which it was suggested, should be present in a learning situation. A fusing of these two, learning characteristics and methods of design are shown in table 5.2, with proposals for integration. A further interpretation is proposed with more specific learning objectives and methods of design.

To briefly highlight these proposals:

- *The lecture and talk* have limitations but are useful for knowledge inputs and should not be ignored.
- *Syndicates/discussions* are seen as particularly useful across the whole range of learning characteristics.
- *Role plays/cases* again are seen as important across the range.
- *In-tray/business game*   Its over-structuring may not cater for individual differences, but again a useful tool.
- *Project*   This comes out quite well, but it suffers from learning plateaux.
- *Algorithms/mnemonics*   Useful aids for recall.
- *Programmed instruction*   A methodical method of learning facts etc.
- *Sensitivity/group/discovery*   They do, by definition, interfere with past learning experiences but the unstructured format makes for 'self learning'.
- *Planned experience*   Critical aspect across the board.
- *Counselling/coaching*   Necessary back-up to the planned experience.

So whatever methods of design we use, we need to be aware of its inner merits and constraints, as well as being able to relate it to wider objectives. We must relate design to these criteria. A range of methods has been given and it is for the individual to select the appropriate technique and related criteria.

On a final note, training aids should be mentioned as part of the design scenario. A note on aids is given in appendix 5F.

We are now equipped to design and develop a learning event, for on- or off-the-job situations. Now we have to put it into practice – and we do so in the next two chapters.

Table 5.2 Proposed relationships between training methods and learning characteristics/objectives

Method	Learning characteristics														Learning objectives				
	1	2	3	4	5	6	7	8	9	10	11	12	13	14	A	B	C	D	E
Lecture				√		√	√		√						•				
Talk	√			√		√	√		√						•	•	•		
Discussion	√	√	√	√	√	√	√	√	√	√	√		√		•	•		•	•
Role play	√	√	√	√	√	√	√		√	√	√		√	√	•	•	•		
Case	√	√	√	√		√	√		√	√	√		√	√	•	•	•	•	•
In-tray	√	√	√	√		√	√		√		√		√	√	•	•			
Business game	√	√	√	√	√	√	√	√			√		√	√	•	•	•	•	•
Project	√	√	√	√		√	√	√	√				√		•	•	•	•	•
Algorithm				√			√		√		√	√	√	√	•				
Mnemonics				√			√		√		√	√	√	√	•				
Programmed instruction				√	√		√		√	√	√	√		√	•		•		
Sensitivity/group	√	√		√	√	√	√		√	√			√		•	•	•	•	•
Discovery learning	√		√	√	√	√	√	√	√	√			√		•		•	•	•
Outdoor training	√		√	√	√	√	√		√	√			√		•	•	•	•	•
Planned experience	√	√	√	√			√	√		√			√	√	•	•	•	•	•
Counselling	√	√	√			√			√	√	√		√		•		•	•	•
Coaching	√	√	√		√	√		√	√		√		√		•		•	•	•

Key

Learning characteristics:
1 Intrinsic motivation
2 Extrinsic motivation
3 Knowledge of results
4 Reward
5 Trial/error
6 'Insightful'
7 Practice
8 Whole learning
9 Part learning
10 Individual differences
11 Period spent/learning plateaux
12 Structured repetition
13 Non-interference with earlier learning
14 Transfer

Learning objectives:
A Knowledge
B Skill
C Use of knowledge/skill
D Attitudes
E Judgement

Appendix 5A   Learner styles, based on Kolb

The 'cycle' is shown below in a little more detail from the learner's perspective:

Concrete experience (CE)

- Subjective/feelings approach to learning.
- Each situation to be treated on own merits.
- Like getting involved.
- Like feedback/discussion with like-minded learners.

Reflective observation (RO)

- Considered/objective approach.
- Observation important.
- May like seminar/lecture as these blend in/facilitate style.

Abstract conceptualization (AC)

- Analytical approach.
- Logic to the fore.
- Theory and systematic analysis is preferred, e.g. major Harvard type case study.

Active experimentation (AE)

- Activity focus.
- Testing in practice.
- May like small group discussion/simulations.

The phases can also give way to a preferred approach emphasizing several of the phases. Some examples are shown below:

'Converger'   (AE and AC) who favours the practical application of ideas and things rather than people. Engineers?

'Diverger'   (CE and RO) who uses imagination and diverse perspectives. Interested in people. Personnel and training managers?

'Assimilator'   (AC and RO) who is into abstract thinking/ideas for themselves. Research/planning?

'Accommodator'   (CE and AE) The action person who is personally involved and who is prepared to take risks. Marketing?

Appendix 5B   Learner situations, based on Honey and Mumford

Situations where the four 'types' learn best:

Activists   Like new experiences and 'here and now' activities such as business games. They like to be in the limelight and doing a task which they see as difficult.

Reflectors   Mulling over activities, using thinking time before action, and taking in information before comment epitomize this approach. They like to review and reflect.

Theorists   Intellectual stimulation, if not stretching, with opportunities to question methods to assumptions one of the hallmarks of this style. The situations are structured and a purpose must exist. Relationships between ideas, events and situations are explored.

Pragmatists   There is a need to relate the subject to the job. A practical emphasis must prevail and opportunities for practice and feedback must exist.

Appendix 5C   Key result areas – How to get them

Step 1   Define role of section/department. That is state the *Purpose* of your unit. Its *raison d'être* and its unique contribution to be noted. For example, to provide a fully trained workforce to meet the operating plan of the organization.

Step 2   Ascertain key result areas for your section/department. For example: increased skills, greater flexibility among employees, greater customer orientation among staff, etc. Relate also to the environment and resources available.

Step 3   Specific KRAs with success criteria to be noted. For example, to increase the skill flexibility of the electricians and plumbers. The criteria can relate to: measurable/quantifiable targets (80 per cent of them achievable; realistic (trade union) pressure); relevant (part of the more flexible firm); manageable (is it down to me? If not under your direct control, then avoid). The criteria can be qualified or quantified.

Step 4   Individual KRAs. The allocation of the key area to the individuals can form the basis of the performance indicators to measure how well they are doing. 'Training gaps' can be determined at the time of review (formal or informal).

Appendix 5D   Training standards

Example: identifying learning needs

- Determine learner competence (individual and group).
- Assess competence.
- Clarify development needs.
- Take account of changes in work role, etc. which impact on perform-ance.
- Clarify individual's long-term aspirations.
- Agree priorities.
- Agree prioritized objectives and learning needs.

Source: Adapted from Training and Development Lead Body, 'How do you spot Good Trainers?'

An example illustrates the 'standard':

Title:	Identify and agree learning strategies that meet client requirements.
Element:	Identify/assess significant learning experience and per-sonal characteristics which influence choice of learning strategy.
Criteria:	– Special needs/circumstances of individuals stated. – Prior learning identified. – Criteria for strategy options created, etc.
Range indicators:	– Prior learning – Personal characteristics. – Methods of Assessment.

Appendix 5E   CRAMP

Learning Type	Some Variables To Consider	Method(s) (examples)
C Understanding/ comprehending	Transfer to many situations Key principles Related past knowledge	Text books Lectures 'Discovery' Basic concepts

R
 Skilled
 (physical)
	Simplify job
	 Planning skills (level)
	 Sequence of tasks
		Simplify tasks
		 Breakdown into
		   progressive steps
		 Discrimination
		   (A versus B, etc.)

Learning Type	Some Variables To Consider	Method(s) (examples)
A Attitude development	Replacement attitudes New attitudes Build on existing attitudes	'Discovery' Role playing Sensitivity/ 'T' groups, etc.
M Knowing what to do (memory)	Relevant job details Length of material Memory 'load'	Rules Structured material Deductive and cumulative parts
P Knowing what to do (relying on relevant information at hand)	Procedural complexity/simplicity Availabilty of material	Checklists Instuctions Algorithms

Source: Adapted from Industrial Training Research Unit, *CRAMP*.

Appendix 5F   Training aids

If the training methods should reflect the learning objectives and content, the training aids should likewise reflect the methods.

Training aids by definition have a function to stimulate and maintain a meaningful learning experience. They assist in reducing complexity, reinforcing the message, facilitating understanding, if not consumption, and gaining and maintaining interest, hence motivation among trainees. For the tutor/trainer/instructor, they help clarify points, act as an *aide mémoire* and can produce a bit of comic relief.

Although they tend to be associated more with off-the-job training, they are useful back-up techniques to on-the-job work as well.

The range is diverse but it includes:

The *chalkboard*, the traditional mainstay of schools, is quite useful for medium sized groups. Preparation before the session can be done by using roller blinds. It has a school teacher – pupil imagery though, and the noise of the chalk on the board can be unbearable. The *white-board* with *felt tips* seems to be preferable for discussions and mini presentations.

The *overhead projector* seems to have displaced the chalkboard in many organizations. It allows the instructor to face the audience and preparation beforehand is not obliterated, unlike with chalk, as transparencies can be used over and over again. It is useful for students/ trainees to give presentations etc. using this method.

Projectors, films, slides and to some extent *tapes/records* have been overtaken by *video/CCTV* (closed circuit television). The advantage of video/CCTV for sound and interpersonal skills seems self-evident, while many proprietary firms produce excellent, if expensive, training videos. *Flipcharts* are useful for brainstorming/discussion sessions. *Photographs* for health and safety, *models* for engineering/construction, *specimens* for biological sciences, *artefacts* for art and *interactive video* for many business uses cover the span of aids.

Interactive video is worth examining in a little more detail. It is comprised of a video set, computer and display screen. In many ways, it is a programmed form of instruction, or programmed learning exploiting technological advances. As a mechanism of learner-based technology it has clear benefits. However, it is only one way of learning and is not suitable for meeting the full range of learning objectives.

Criteria for using aids must be noted. The work of R. H. Anderson concerning media selection and usage can be cited:

- Aids should be necessary to make things *easier*.
- They should be *simple* and large enough to *understand*.
- Layout should stimulate *interest*.
- The aids should be suitable to the needs.[12]

At the end of the day, aids must relate to methods and total learning objectives, which has been the theme of this chapter.

Notes

1 For example, see D. A. Kolb, 'Towards an applied theory of experiential learning'.
2 It may be that in more abstract thinking, as in higher education and in aspects of non-routine management, the 'experience' model may not really apply. The baseline may be concept and theory first and then testing through experience with appropriate modifications to the initial concept and so on (see below).

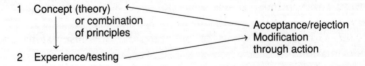

3 See P. Honey and A. Mumford, *A Manual of Learning Styles.*

4 M. Kubr, 'Principles for the selection of teaching and training methods'.

5 E. Donnelly, 'The Training Model: Time for a change?'

6 See M. Thakur, J. Bristow and K. Carby, *Personnel in Change – Organisation Development through the Personnel Function.*

7 R. Mager, *Preparing Instructional Objectives.*

8 R. Coverdale. For example, existing training courses of the consultancy, such as *The Practice of Teamwork*, Parts I, II and III.

9 D. Laird, *Approaches to Training and Development.*

10 S. Carroll et al., 'The relative effectiveness of training methods – expert opinion and research'.

11 J. G. Burgoyne, T. Boydell and M. Pedler, *Self Development, Theory and Applications for Practitioners.*

12 R. H. Anderson, 'Selection of media: another perspective'. See also A. J. Romiszowski, *The Selection and Use of Instructional Media.*

6
Implementation

Objectives

- To put into effect the administrative arrangements for training implementation.
- To understand the relationships between on-the-job and off-the-job training.
- To make meaningful selections on implementation methods of on-the-job training.
- To make meaningful recommendations/selections on implementation methods for off-the-job training.

Implementation
Life is not long enough to keep retracing the path and discussing where we should have gone. The experience of going wrong is the real lesson ... Perhaps the greatest gift is the ability to stand away and view yourself and the situation from the outside. Being self-critical achieves little on its own. Changing the criticisms into actions is satisfying and reaps its own rewards.

Two delegates, Steve and Larry,
who attended an outdoor training session.
Quoted by J. Teire, 'Using the outdoors'.

Overview

Putting the design into practice is the 'doing' or implementation stage. This phase can be divided into two steps:

1 Practical administrative arrangements are required – from making and communicating details of programmes to recording and writing up the details after completion on some training record system.[1] Where staff trainers exist, this role tends to lie with them.

2 Carrying out the training is the main aspect and it is the subject of this unit.

The implementation phase itself is not only dependent on the design and needs stages, but it must be consistent with the organizational priorities established by the training policy and, more significantly, the training plan. So we need a brief consideration of training policies and plans.

The main themes in this unit are.

- Implementation will depend on a pragmatic approach towards 'plans' as well as the pure approach derived from needs and design.
- The system behind doing on-the-job or off-the-job training is similar in concept.
- The line trainer has a key role in on-the-job training.
- Off-the-job training should be a shared process between line staff trainers.
- External resources and agencies must dovetail into the specific learning needs of the organization and its 'culture'.

Training Policies

As we have already looked at the link between corporate planning and manpower/human resource planning in chapter 4, little time will be spent on this interface here.[2] Suffice to say, the innovative work of Walker gives a useful summary of the links between Corporate Planning and Human Resource Planning (see box 6.1).[3]

The training policy is the training link between the function and HR planning. Written statements of training policy are often bland, meaningless documents written for internal public relations consumption. They can have value, if indicative of a real commitment to training, by:

- Reducing ambiguities over the main thrust of training.
- Enhancing the standing of training *vis à vis* other functions with their policies.
- Being a potential tool of selling training to the non-believers – particularly in a highly structured and authoritarian organization.

Policy statements tend to note the aims and specific approaches to implementing these aims with some allocation of responsibilities to managers. It *may* include such items as:

- A statement confirming the value of training to organizational efficiency.
- The obligations of the organization to provide training.

Box 6.1   Human resource planning/strategic planning

CORPORATE PLAN

Strategic planning: Long-range perspective	Operational planning: Middle-range perspective	Budgeting: Annual perspective
Corporate philosophy	Planned programmes	Budgets
Environmental scan Strengths & constraints	Resources required Organizational strategies	Unit, individual performance goals
Objectives & goals	Plans for entry into new businesses, acquisitions, divestitures	Programme scheduling and assignment
Strategies		Monitoring and control of results

HUMAN RESOURCE PLAN

Issue Analysis	Forecasting requirements	Action plans
Business needs	Staffing levels	Staffing authorization
External factors	Staffing mix (qualitative)	Recruitment
Internal supply analysis	Organization and job design	Promotions and transfers
Management implications	Available/projected resources	Organizational changes
	Net requirements	*Training and development
		Compensation and benefits
		Labour relations

Source: Adapted from J. W. Walker, 'Linking HR Planning and Strategic Planning'.

- Priorities or critical areas of implementation – e.g. new, transferred and promoted people to be trained; initial skills training for all; the link (if any) to the appraisal scheme and the importance of the needs analysis; the type of methods/techniques to be used (global) and the link to continuing education for all.
- Staff involved (job titles).

See box 6.2 for an example.

The Training Plan

This plan takes a forward look at training, perhaps over a year, and sets parameters and priorities for the implementation stage. Typical general questions, together with their relationships to training systems are:

1 What type of training is required? – See needs analysis and design/ learning.

Box 6.2   Example of a training policy

Definition:	Of training and link to development.
Purpose of policy:	1 Increase organizational efficiency through skills/ knowledge etc. 2 Develop individual capacities.
Specific objectives:	1 To meet job requirements and agreed standards of performance. 2 To provide vocational skills hence ensuring eligibility for transfer/promotion. 3 Induction to be carried out. 4 To carry out initial training for new staff. 5 To train staff who are promoted/transferred. 6 To ensure appraisal and counselling systems are maintained.
Responsibilities:	Of managers (staff/line). Central, divisional and local role of group training services.
Further education:	Open University, day release fees, examination leave, etc.

2 Why is it required? – Internal/external justification, evaluation and needs analysis.
3 Who are the people involved? – Needs analysis.
4 What resources etc. are required? – Design/budgets etc.
5 What are the most pressing or critical areas? – Relate to policy and pressures from needs related to resources available.
6 How, when and where will it be carried out and by whom? – Implementation phase.[4]

At this stage, a developed record system for training comes into its own.

Implementing Training

The normal division for implementation occurs between on-the-job and off-the-job training. As it sounds, training 'on the job' takes place at the workbench, factory or office. 'Off-the-job' training is removed from the place of work, for example to a seminar room.

Training off the job is easier to control, 'safer' with errors having no impact on operational efficiency, and it is less random with variables interfering with training being minimized. It can be unrealistic, however, and the problems of learning transfer from training centre to workplace are legend.

Training on the job allows easier transfer of learning, but it is less safe as errors may cause problems in this 'real' situation. It is probably cheaper but it does suffer from 'a baptism under fire' approach, and the cheaper aspect of training can prove to be a lot more expensive at the end of the day if there is unsystematic training.

Findings from the UK Training Agency's survey gives a cost/time perspective.[5] Some 64.7 million days of off the job training occurred in the survey period (in the late 1980s) compared to 60.7 million days of on the job training. On average, each employee received some seven days training per year (3.6 days off the job and 3.4 days of on the job). Of course, the figures are distorted as more than 50 per cent of employees received no training at all. Qualification of on the job training may be quite difficult for 'sitting watching Nellie' may not be seen as 'real' training.[6]

One of the themes of this book is that the line manager is, in effect, a line trainer, and so a lot of the implementation will fall to him or her – particularly on-the-job training – but he or she will have important inputs into off-the-job training as well. One of the themes of this chapter on implementation is that the learning implementation strategy is not dissimilar between on-the-job and off-the-job training and the training system advocated in this text is applicable to both methods. Both need a programme, although the on-the-job one would be less formalized and probably less detailed, showing indicative content only. Both need the objectives, timing, content/format and notes on equipment, materials or aids with a 'map' of the sub-objectives which need to be met. An example is shown in box 6.3.

So this task could be adapted for a specific part of an off-the-job programme, a seminar, open learning, or a structured on-the-job programme with more of a rolling deadline. Hence we have ignored aids/materials etc. as they will differ according to method of implementation. So the principles are seen as very similar: *task, objective(s), main content and skills with some acknowledgement to constraints* such as time, equipment, resources, etc. The line and staff trainer must approach the learning implementation in a structured format. This approach is applicable to the traditional techniques/methods of both on-the-job and off-the-job training.[7]

Box 6.3 On/off-the-job training – a similar process

Task:	Managing a small firm
Overall aim:	To illustrate the importance of goal setting.
Main activity:	To draw up an objective/goal-setting guide for your small firm.
Content to be covered:	1 Selling goals.
	2 Target setting.
	3 Mission statements.
	4 MBO.
Learner activity:	1 Goals – Self examination of strengths. Apply to a real 'case' or scenario. Test the self strengths/business success equation.
	2 Targets – Must be able to conduct a 'strength/weakness/opportunity/threat' analysis for own firm. Present some to staff/line trainer.
	3 Mission – Clarify hierarchy of objectives for the firm. Write a mission statement/sub-objectives for the firm.
	4 MBO – Research concept. Apply this target setting system to your firm and write up functional objectives.
Skills:	Problem solving/design analysis; processing information once gathered; numeracy and communicating.

Source: Extract from Anderson Associates', Training Programme for Small Firms and Owner/Managers

---

On-the-job training

There is a range of methods from a very directed style of approach with tight constraints and little room to manoeuvre to a more *laissez faire*, self-developmental programme with the individual coming to the fore to meet agreed initial objectives.

'Sitting by Nellie'[8]

This means watching an experienced 'pair of hands' at work. The proficient can make difficult things look easy and although it is a cheap method, much depends on the competence of, and the 'trainer' potential of, 'Nellie'. Bad habits can also be picked up – see how many unconscious mistakes an 'experienced' driver makes. If Nellie has objectives etc. and knows how to instruct, life is simpler.

Telling/selling

Essentially a verbal explanation of 'how to do'. Back-up illustrations or a workbook can be used for more complex tasks. It is better if it is not just one way, so question and answer sessions at the end may be useful.

Formal demonstration

Again still very much a 'teacher–pupil' relationship but useful for imparting the operation of a new process or new machine.

Job or task (depending on complexity) instruction

This is really a continuation of the task analysis that we have seen before. It can be used in a one-to-one situation or to a group undertaking the same job (e.g. new starts to a warehouse). This is a useful method as the individual trainee is involved in the process. See box 6.4. This is a good step by step method whereby every action is listed, arranged in a logical manner and special learning points are reinforced. Again, equipment in use is noted.

Supervised practice

This gives the trainee some rope to learn but the rope is still being held by the line trainer. An example is a newspaper office where telesales advertising reps are listened to by the line trainer during discussions with potential buyers. This allows speed and confidence to be built up progressively, but the supervisor should adapt a trainer role rather than that of a performance-led manager to encourage 'growth' of the trainee.

A practical lesson will involve instruction, action from the trainee and more informal 'walkabout' by the line trainer.

Discussions

These provide a periodic review of events, such as weekly meetings where past and future workloads can be examined. This in many

---

Box 6.4   Example of the 'job instruction' method

Aim: To introduce new starters to 'goods in' procedures.
Location: Storeroom.
Scenario: Vehicle arrives at 'back door' of shop and unloads pallets/
             crates and signs into warehouse.
Step 1:   Code each 'piece' of load.
             Equipment – refer to coding manual.
             Key points – Able to distinguish 'grocery' from textiles' etc.
Step 2:   Locate 'goods received register'.
             Equipment – Use computer printout.
             Key points – Check with 'goods in' warehouse person
               that the goods tally.
Step 3:   Pricing procedures.
             Equipment – Use 'gun', sticker labels and price lists (up to
               date)
             Key points – Check size/product etc with up-to-date price
               list and set 'gun' accordingly etc.

---

ways is an extension of ongoing coaching of the individual by perhaps reviewing progress and highlighting areas for action. It is time-consuming and is the basis of the time-honoured tradition of the apprentice serving the master. The mentoring process is an extension of this process. Mentoring has a connotation of 'sponsorship' reminiscent of the Florentine Renaissance with aspiring artists and rich protectors. It has a political overtone as well, as with the mentor perhaps opening doors for his or her protégé. If the tasks are planned and some *counselling* exists between the trainer and trainee, this scheme has some merit, but it can degenerate into some political sponsorship. A non-judgemental feedback discussion allied to good counselling skills is a useful method of resetting learning objectives and giving new directions to learning. This may be related to a career development discussion.

A performance-based appraisal scheme may set objectives but it is not really a 'safe' learning vehicle as salary increases, promotion, and maybe discipline, may be riding on the outcome of the appraisal. So training/development should be differentiated from the performance/salary aspect of the appraisal.

The trainee, once briefed with clear objectives, can be usefully given assignments as the representative of the group/section/department at monthly meetings, from budgets to planning, or asked to join project teams for a specific time-scale.

So we have moved from the instructional approach through to practice and on to the interactive 'live' attempt. In this spectrum the line trainer's immediate control is decreasing and giving the individual trainee more control over his or her own learning, although the line trainer is still there 'floating' in the background and giving support.

Other methods increase the independence of the trainee. Job rotation, job swaps or changes for a short time, and covering a job in the vacation or deputizing for a peer or boss will give greater exposure to the roles and tasks of others. Self-development programmes, from using open learning packages to self-initiated learning, complete this process. Perhaps above all else, at this end of the spectrum, the 'live' project or action report is an excellent way of combining themes of self learning in a practical context. Action learning would seem to be an under-used activity and could be spread to non-managerial jobs as well.[9]

Before leaving on-the-job training (and this list is not exhaustive), there should be mention of *some* on-the-job training aids. *Algorithms* or flow charts giving some fishbone type of analysis are helpful for fault finding, and mnemonics, such as CRAMP (see chapter 3) act as an *aide mémoire*. Action replays on a video or film slow down the learning tasks into a stepped or part learning approach. Interactive video allows the individual to work at a given pace and is good for increasing product knowledge or language skills.[10] Training manuals on 'how to do' should not be forgotten, although they are 'lower tech'. These aids are mainly reference sources for the learner – excluding interactive video which is more of a mainstream technique that by definition can be programmed and is more programmable and responsive to learner needs.

Discovery learning gives even more of a trainee-oriented approach. In reality it is less unstructured than at first glance as parameters are set out, although the trainee has considerable scope within these limits. It is self-directed learning within a 'plan' held by the line or staff trainer. It is time-consuming, though, and trainees may feel that they are being used as guinea-pigs, so they need to be aware of the aims and principles behind the process.

The aim goes back to a view of learning whereby learner activity is prized, self-initiated work is seen as best remembered, and relevance is taken from finding out or 'discovering' rather than being 'instructed'. It may have some value with bright trainees – possibly young graduates – who will 'play the game'. Mature individuals may not appreciate the concept and may be put off by the 'gamesmanship' element. Some of these problems may be overcome by knowledge of the 'principles' of learning:

- The instructor/tutor/manager must have a 'plan of action' related to the overall learning objectives.
- This is best achieved by a plan of questions (open-ended). Some flexibility should be in-built to counter obstacles.
- The questioning is 'progressive' and 'guided'.
- The learner must trust the tutor.
- The learner needs to be aware of the concept discovery approach.
- The learner sets his or her own pace.
- This type of approach is seen to be useful to 'comprehension' type of learning.
- The individual learner is given much rope to 'discover' the techniques/ principles etc. which will lead to understanding of the whole concept or process.
- Unobtrusive stimulation of the learner should occur and questions by the learner should be met by questions.
- Silent observation of the learner is encouraged and demonstrations by the tutor/manager should be discouraged.

Off-the-job training

This is not just about attendance at a training course. It covers a range of activities from mountaineering to directed reading to going to a conference. Further, ostensibly non-training situations can be used for off-the-job training as well. So, using these 'pure' and 'hijacked' categories we can examine some of the options. Before we do this though, it should be reiterated that such training is *not* the sole preserve of the staff trainer.

Courses and skill workshops

These are useful when common needs have been identified. They facilitate staff getting together – perhaps from other sections, or indeed other organizations (see later) and training occurs in a 'safe' place away from the pressures of work. If distractions are minimized, transfer back to work must be maximized by a combination of theory and practice and the inputs must be realistic and based on

---

Box 6.5   Effective lecturing: principles

Tutor/lecturer: Off-the-job 'inputs'

The line trainer may be called upon to have some input into an off-the-job training event. It is most unlikely that this will be a 'pure' lecture in its literal sense. There may be 'instruction' but there will also be audience involvement – either during or at the end of the session.

Principles

- Do not give any input unless you really know your stuff. You may not be called to use it all, but you need to know it.
- Do prepare beforehand and even rehearse it (time allowing) with a tape recorder.
- Do have a plan, with aims, a body and a conclusion.
- Do use notes/overheads as appropriate but they are *aids* not crutches for the input.
- Do be careful with humour: the place for comedians may not be in the training centre.
- Do get the right 'pitch' for your audience and use language that trainees can understand and relate to.
- Do be prepared to alter your plan (hence solid preparation beforehand) provided that you finally meet your learning objectives.
- Do remember the principles of learning and apply them.

---

sound learning principles. As a line trainer you may have to recommend people for such events. Your role is to ensure that:

- Trainees have common needs.
- The course/workshop meets these needs.
- The trainee is prepared, so discuss the session with trainees *prior* to the event so that their expectations have got the right 'pitch'.
- The post-course follow-up should not be neglected.

In the event, you may be called upon to be a 'guest' lecturer.[11] See box 6.5 for some pointers.

As a line trainer many of the other options may be guided by the staff trainer, so your role is to be aware of the range, and the respective pros and cons of each method as they impact upon your

---

Box 6.6   Outdoor development – an example

Title: Night exercise
Purpose(s): To test established plans of the group in conducting themselves in an orderly manner. To reinforce the need for a sound structure (objectives/plans) upon which to build. To facilitate group integration and people helping one another.
Scene: Conducted entirely in the dark.
Situation: This is the last in a series of objectives/planning exercises. Two groups are sent on a mission to 'enemy' territory. Full briefing given. Groups dropped at different locations. They should make their respective ways to a hilltop. They pick up messages on the way at a 'safe' house in a wooded area where they exchange information and plan the final 'assault'.

---

training needs. It may be useful to add some comments against a range of methods (again, the list is not exhaustive).

Outdoor development

This is taking people away from work and putting them in some mountainous region. Some call it training in 'life skills' development:

> ... while conventional education refines and stretches the mind, extramural education reaches out to the spirit. And since spirit influences mind, the argument runs, non-academic education can subtly alter professional capacity and social behaviour.   (I. Cranfield, *Training Through Endeavour*.)

Teire gives a succinct rationale for going outdoors: the realism is self-evident; the situations and problems require real solutions; the radical change of environment can 'shake us out of our ruts'; and it involves feelings and actions – both individual and group.[12]

An example of outdoor development is shown in box 6.6.

Attachments

Putting people out of the office or factory need not be as dramatic as the box 6.6 exercise. Fieldtrips from headquarters to sites within the firm are extremely useful during induction periods. Trips to other firms and countries can be useful for operators, technicians and senior managers to view new machines and systems etc. Selected individuals can visit, thus reducing costs. Trade secrecy may inhibit such events, but employers' associations and the DTI etc. may help.

Some sort of study-leave or sabbatical, as occurs in academic environments, or conducting a specific work-related project within companies or whatever may be worth considering for the likes of R & D people. Attaching liaison people to consultants and advisers to the firm may act as a training session. For example, may years ago while with British Gas I worked closely with consultants from the Institute of Manpower Studies who were installing a system of occupational classification. Fresh viewpoints and close internal management involvement can follow from this approach.

Individual initiatives

Increasingly open learning is being used in training. This is self-paced and directed within given parameters. Once running, it is cheap (relatively), flexible and allows short 'bursts' of learning. However, the initial capital expense, the lack of the expert tutor, and its inability to meet all learning styles may be seen as the negative aspect of this approach. It does work though, and two interesting applications are:

1 In the retail organization, 'Q', many stores have started to use interactive video which allows self-pacing by the trainee and is aimed at increasing product knowledge and heightened awareness of health and safety issues.
2 A leading insurance company, 'The Mutual', has developed an interactive system to train sales personnel. It is comprised of a series of interactive video and computer-based packages and is aimed at stimulating positive feedback and response.

Guided reading, references to current magazines and an on-site video library for videos on business issues may be conducive for self-learning. Continuing education may also be related to this activity, but this moves away from the self-developmental work-based activity into more esoteric educational areas

Group initiatives

The engineer can be selected for a project team, either inside or outside of the place of work. Depending upon the nature of the project and its duration, this may be on-the-job or off-the-job training.

Brainstorming and away days can be used for getting ideas together and for action points. It may be useful to have an outside facilitator for these. Personal experience with a leading British airline at Heathrow proved this to a useful team setting, where the group expressed their views and attitudes (via structured questionnaires) and feedback was given. Traditionally, a conference is used for sales staff and for senior managers. Other functions could usefully benefit from these sessions as an integrative theme, 'a state of the nation', a planning theme, or whatever, so long as there is a theme with good guest speakers and facilitators.

Non-training initiatives

The idea here is that the normal work processes provide a learning situation and off-the-job work activities may also provide learning facilities. For example, the appraisal scheme may provide a free flow of ideas and information and can highlight individual developmental programmes. Quality circles or quality teams may facilitate a group problem-solving situation which encourages group integration and open communications. Assessment and developmental centres *may* be a learning exercise, as the focus is on-the-job and success criteria for particular jobs. Unfortunately, if it degenerates into a pressurized promotion platform, as they often do, the training will be submerged by the assessment aspect.

In this review we should not forget the 'half-way houses' between on the off-the-job training. Vestibule training provides a simulated workshop for technicians, flight simulators and artificial cockpits train aspiring pilots, and both replicate the job environment without the disadvantages of the reality of work pressures and the possibility of accidents etc.

One further thought that should be developed is that of action learning, as it does bridge the gap between theory and practice, between on and off-the-job training, and between training and education.

It is geared to management and, by definition, its focus is on activity that is doing rather than diagnosing and analysing *per se*. It is problem-based and hence demands a solution. So there is some analysis and reflection but it is a practical and workable project that is at stake. Learning significance means, according to this view, that it should have a specific meaning for the individual learner. Finally it is a dynamic concept and builds on, and demands, 'shared' learning between groups of learners.

Apart from the 'group think' mentality and an action man rather than thinking man rationale, it can be of benefit to organizations. Perhaps another approach, in part a type of spin-off from this concept, would be the assignment/project. It would not have to be just 'given' to managers as, for example, junior administrators/clerks and technicians could usefully employ this tool. It needs to be problem-oriented, it can have more of a research flair to it with a more rigorous methodology building upon past experiences and the research/literature of others; the method would reflect the nature of the problem; and recommendations would follow. It would be the work of one individual who has a 'tutor', and the tutor should be the line or staff trainer. This is moving more towards an educational project, not a dissertation as such, and must have practical applications to the organization, to the trainee and to the tutor.

Internal or External Resources?

For the last eighteen years I have been involved with human resource management/training both in an internal capacity, working for an organization as an employee, and as an external adviser working with the organization but as an outsider. So I can objectively deal with both visions.

It should not be internal resource versus external resource, for the outsiders are there to supplement and complement the internal initiatives. The criteria for judging both types of resource are the same: cost effectiveness. In addition, when contemplating external assistance their objecting and 'wordly wisdom' must be balanced by cost and organizational relevance. The oft quoted survey, *Training in Britain*, gives some employers' views on choosing training providers.[13] The following list gives the percentage of those questioned as saying these factors were important in choosing training providers:

Level of expertise	66%
Quality	44%
Breadth of experience	41%
Flexibility of provision	28%
Value for money	24%
Geographical location	20%
Reputation of provider	12%
Cost	12%
Previous contact	11%

Management recommendation	10%
Tradition	5%

Thankfully, quality and expertise were considered by the majority of employers as important. As the internal resource has been covered, a brief note on some of the external supplements is necessary. The main ones are: seminars/courses, colleges/business schools, conferences, consultants and packages.

Mailshots descend upon our desks advertising 'open' seminars and courses from leadership to quality assurance. These 'public' seminars are open to all, so your need must link with their provision. New ideas, mixing with other individuals possibly from different sectors may be a refreshing change but the real criterion is need, and does the seminar meet your needs?

Costs tend not to be the same problem at business schools. Like the seminar market, they seemed to mushroom during the 1970s and 1980s, with many underfunded colleges of higher education and polytechnics starting 'schools of business' with their own Masters degrees. While they may remain the poorer relation of the older establishments and others ask if 'MBA' means 'more bad advice', they have a role to play. Junior managers and administrators can benefit from day-release facilities for professional qualifications and diplomas; middle, functional type managers can broaden out with appropriate general qualifications, such as the DMS; and senior managers can gain from seminars in strategy and policy etc. They may be financially undemanding on your budget compared to 'open' seminars but often the schools have a knowledge base, rather than a skills base, and the poverty of educational resources in the UK means that it is worth checking out the faculty and its members as well as the resources, library and computing, which they can offer.

Conferences are less cheap but they provide a useful terminological 'cover' for training as many senior people by definition of their position may feel that they are beyond training.

External consultants can be used by organizations as a mechanism of bringing external resources into their milieu, hence cultural problems, in theory, should be minimized, assuming the consultant can switch 'in' to the new culture. Objectivity and skill coupled to experience of other industries and firms may benefit the organization. You should seek formal proposals on fees and should avoid firms selling packages, irrespective of the client's real needs. The costs can be quite significant, with some partners in City firms charging some £1670 in 1990 for their *daily* charge-out rate to clients.

A tremendous range of packages and training material from videos to instructor programmes to books are available in this area and, again, needs must be uppermost in the mind of the buyer, balanced by cost, of course.

So external resources can give expertise, an objective vision with no political axe to grind and a fresh perspective. Costs need to be examined in the context of the offerings from outside. The external assistance must also be integrated with your learning objectives and specific programme needs to be beneficial. This is one reason why some consultants tend not to do 'open' programmes.

Implementation Strategies

A brief note is required on implementation strategy. Jones used the term 'intervention' to describe access into the 'vital processes' of the organization.[14] The staff trainer should become an active innovator who can relate business and training needs to one another. Jones really is advocating an organization-wide vision with the staff specialist taking an opportunistic–entrepreneurial role in looking for openings for training. In addition, though, a professional line trainer concept as advocated here will facilitate such openings and reduce the selling role of the trainer.

Implementation Skills

The line trainer must have a working understanding of the range of off-the-job 'solutions' and the merits of external assistance. The line trainer must have a sound knowledge of the on-the-job solutions and of the 'real politic' in which he or she operates, particularly concerning resources.

However, the line trainer has an enormous role to play in implementing training on the job and in recommending off-the-job training, coupled to providing learning opportunities and transfer of knowledge/skills when the trainee returns to work after a spell of off-the-job training.

Clearly a policy and 'plan of campaign' give a vision to this phase.

Whether it is off the job, or on, or some combination, the principles of operating are similar, although the techniques and methods differ greatly.

Notes

1 PPITB (Printing and Publishing Industry Training Board) *Training Records – An Aid to Sound Company Training*.
2 The definitions of 'manpower' or 'human resource' or 'personnel management' seem to trouble many people. See D. Guest's interesting review 'Personnel and HRM: Can you tell the difference?'.
3 J. W. Walker, 'Linking HR planning and strategic planning'.
4 This list comes from Anderson Associates, Research and Management Advisors, 7 Water Lane, Melbourn, Herts, UK. This training and developing firm has been owned by Maureen Anderson since 1982.
5 Training Agency, *Training in Britain*.
6 M. Sloman makes some interesting points on the need for an integrated approach to on-the-job training. See 'On The Job Training – a costly poor relation'.
7 D. Celinski argued for a more systematic approach to the whole concept. See 'Systematic on the job training'.
8 The degree to which trainee behaviour can be 'modelled' on established criteria is pursued by D. Grant in 'A better way of learning from Nellie'.
9 See M. Pedler, *Action Learning in Practice* and the classical work of R. Revans, *The ABC of Action Learning*.
10 See Institute of Personnel Management factsheet, *Interactive Video*.
11 An excellent book on 'how to lecture' written from an educational perspective which may have to be 'diluted' for mature adults in training is: University Teaching Methods Unit, *Improving Teaching in Higher Education*.
12 J. Teire, 'Using the outdoors'.
13 Training Agency, *Training in Britain*.
14 J. A. G. Jones, *Training Intervention Strategies*.

7

Outputs

Objective

To establish implementation programmes or 'outputs' at four levels of 'intervention':

1 individual;
2 job;
3 function;
4 organization.

One after the other, on both sides of the Atlantic, bits and pieces of the Japanese formula have been tried: quality circles, Total Quality Management, Just-in-Time, time based management and so forth. But the suspicion has intensified that the parts are much less important than the whole: that success lies less in what the Japanese do than in their persistence in doing it.

R. Heller, 'The Change Managers'.

Overview

Our systems approach has looked at the inputs and the transformation processes making for the outputs. We have also considered the nature of the implementation process. This chapter will consolidate the work of chapter 6 and give in-depth illustrative examples of the end product of the whole system.

The focus, as in our systems model, will be on four levels of intervention with appropriate examples:

1 Individual level – induction for the newcomer.
2 Job level – supervisory training.
3 Functional level (i.e. subject focus) – industrial relations, training.
4 Organizational level – training as part of the management of change.

In reality, specific training needs will dictate most of the content of this chapter. In the absence of such needs, the results from research and personal experiences are given.

Induction Training

Induction training is concerned with integrating the new employee into the job and organization as quickly as possible. So it is an initiation, a transition between the unknown and the more familiar, and it is part of what sociologists would term the 'socialization' process.[1] This initial period of adjustment should benefit both the newcomer and the organization by the following:

- The individual 'settles down' and makes a quicker transition into the job and the organization.
- The reduction of labour turnover may result, as the first few months of the job are critical in the decision to stay or leave.
- The employee becomes better informed on organizational structure, policies and procedures etc., so the formal rules are known.
- The informal rules and intricacies of 'what is what around here' helps the culturalization process.

The line trainer has a key input into this induction process assisted by the personnel department, if it exists.

The induction programme is for all new starts filling existing positions or newly established jobs. In theory, it should apply to both permanent and temporary newcomers, but the time and energy spend on temps will be less. Two groups which may need a lot of time are school and college leavers. Often they have particular difficulties in adjusting to a working environment. The longer hours, the discipline of work, a change of status from education to work, and new relationships and responsibilities all add to this difficulty of transition.

The line trainer with assistance from the personnel department must be able to structure the content of the programme and to deliver it to the newcomers. The content of the programme can be separated into various segments: organization; terms and conditions; policies and procedures; health, safety and welfare; departmental session(s); the job; customer/client sensitivity; normative analysis, e.g. quality; training and development.

Organization – factual information

Much of the contextual information on the organization – its products/services and its brief history – can be handled by using a handbook. As this will be for *all* employees the information should be contextual and general. The handbook can be circulated to the new employee alongside the offer of appointment prior to the person joining the firm. This general handbook should include the following details:

- The *background* to the organization – without being a thesis.
- The *industry setting* – with some reference to the make-up of the industry sector and its general characteristics.
- The *organization's place* in that sector – a general statement should suffice as market share/profitability etc. will *not* be required. For more senior people this can be picked up later and company reports etc. can be given.
- The *product/service* range with some past contacts/examples of work to give a 'feel' for what the organization actually does.
- A 'who's who' of the organization can be an appendix in the booklet, or a loose sheet; or perhaps it is even best left until a later discussion, as these personalities may change too quickly for economic publication.

Terms/conditions

These are the formal agreements and rules binding the parties together. The contractual terms may have been outlined at the initial interviews and in the letter of appointment, but they should be reinforced at the outset – probably at day one by the personnel department or line trainer.

The agreement should cover: salary/wage information; bonus; overtime; shift and other payments and the mechanics of payment; holiday arrangements; sick pay and absence procedures; trade union agreements, if applicable; and any other aspects of remuneration and benefits. As this will probably be individualized, it is best dealt with on a one-to-one basis. Grievances over terms and conditions cause great problems, so there should be no ambiguity right from the outset.

Policies and procedures, rules and regulations

People need to know where they stand. If smoking is banned, this should be made clear from the beginning. These critical rules should be written up beforehand and incorporated in a clear format into a looseleaf type of folder for new employees. Policies such as security and confidentiality need to be noted. The policies on discipline, and searching people, for example, need to be incorporated into this file. Moreover, the organization should not come across as a nit-picking, rule-bound bureaucracy. At the same time, key rules need to be made clear with the manager highlighting the *critical* rules.

It is important not to throw too much at the individual immediately, as the learning curve will be quite rapid with learning reaching a plateau very quickly. For managers who have to implement policies and procedures or 'standing instructions' a separate session some weeks later will be required as part of their individual training.

Health, safety and welfare

Some industries and jobs are more hazardous than others and in these health and safety will be writ large. In this context, an input session/lecture by the safety officer should occur certainly in the first week, and preferably before the individual is allowed unsupervized among the potential hazards.

For less hazardous industries or jobs, health and safety should still merit attention to keep potential hazards at bay. This would include: fire prevention and procedures; first aid and location of boxes and first aiders; the role of the safety officer and the inspectorate; and accident causation/prevention. Certainly this merits some discussion and information to add to the looseleaf binder.

Hygiene, from barrier creams to long hair and machines, particularly in the food and drink sectors, needs special attention. Again, standards of dress, personal cleanliness, jewellery hazards, etc. need to be highlighted to all staff, from machinery operators to salespeople.

This also should occur within the first week and lends itself to a talk or a video (if the volume of newcomers or industry type) demands such a process.

The individual's welfare is also important. This lends itself more to the departmental session once the individual physically starts the work. This would cover canteen or restaurant, cloakrooms, special clothing and sports and social facilities, etc.

Departmental session(s)

Once these general policies, procedures and contractual arrangements have been carried through, the individual(s) should have a tour of relevant departments which he or she will be coming in contact with in everyday work.

The various departmental heads or supervisors can explain the functions of 'their' departments and specific equipment, machines, methods noted as they go on. This type of visitation should occur once the person has been assigned to a department section, and then the visits should occur once the individual has a feel for his or her own workplace. This should occur within the first few weeks and it needs careful organizing by the line trainer so that the newcomer has some programme to follow.

The individual needs to get bedded down in the right section, usually after the initial discussion on the first day with the personnel and safety people. The line trainer has a key role here, illustrating how the department blends into the organizational jigsaw, the specific aims and objectives coupled to a 'who's who' of the section (in an objective fashion). The individual can be introduced to work colleagues and the union representative, if applicable, on day one. Role and cultural expectations will enter the scene at this stage. We will return to this subject.

The job

Clearly the individual is there to do a job of work. Depending upon the newcomer's past experiences, a brief programme may be required. Even qualified personnel need to be aware of the organizational jargon, shortcuts and procedures. The line trainer can list the learning objectives and have a scheme of work for the newcomer. An experienced 'mentor' is priceless in showing the ropes to the newcomers, and the training programme can be adapted and adopted to meet such relationships.

Customer/client sensitivity

'Customer care' programmes abound, particularly in many newly privatized and existing public sector organizations. The 'customer is king' philosophy permeates such organizations, so this view needs

to be there at the beginning, reflected in the policies, procedures and attitudes of management, even though the customer contact is indirect.

Normative analysis

The customer orientation is only one positive 'norm' that organizations may wish to imbue into their new entrants. We know that
the 'informal' organization[2] and group norms may tell against the
espoused policies of management. This seems inevitable – but the
'formal' organization has a good opportunity to put its case in
the first few weeks of operation. The 'core value' system of Peters
and Waterman can be cited as an example of the formal system.[3]
Others have tried to look at effectiveness from other perspectives
and have come to similar conclusions, one of which is that positive
norms do make for greater effectiveness.[4] The induction period is
crucial in coming to terms with these new norms.

Training and development

The line trainer as a line manager should have been involved in the
selection procedure. Very few people meet the job specification in its
entirety, so training and developmental needs as well as personnel,
job and career orientations and plans need to be discussed.

Unless the individual does not really meet the job specification
(and if so, why was that person selected?) 'top up' training may be
required. This needs an objective analysis by the line trainer/
manager using the job schedule/priorities for the initial training
review, which must take place within the first month – assuming
some basic competency. If not competent, this occurs very early of
course. Discussion on training facilities, educational opportunities,
the appraisal system (if applicable) and career developmental 'chats'
should wait until the person has been in the organization for some
months.

The immediate training, on and off the job, may be more of a
priority – see the chapter on training needs analysis (chapter 4). Box
7.1 summarizes this section on induction in the form of a checklist.

First Level Management/Supervisory Training

The first line manager performs a difficult job, as this postholder is
the representative of management and has daily contact with the

---

Box 7.1 Principles of induction checklist

☐ Use other sections and key personnel such as the shop steward, personnel and safety officer, etc.

☐ Don't overdo it – we reach a learning peak quite early in a new environment.

☐ Be flexible. Some school-leavers will need a fair bit of induction while experienced managers may need only context, policies and procedures, etc.

☐ Try to use a mentor or an experienced person that the newcomer can shadow.

☐ Be ruthless with the information inputs – some things are critical others 'nice to know'.

☐ Use one-to-one methods for personal discussions and group inputs for things such as safety lectures.

☐ Induction is not basic training and we should try to separate the two.

☐ Remember, newly promoted people and transfers-in may not need the organizational input, but they still need part induction.

☐ The induction is a good tool of establishing the positive norms of the place.

☐ A manual or handbook is useful, in the form of a looseleaf binder.

☐ Some follow up (by the personnel department) after three months is useful.

☐ Have a plan of campaign.

---

workforce. Often this manager has come from the workgroup itself, is bypassed by shop stewards who go to the next level of management, and ignored by more senior managerial colleagues. Yet this job should be a key part of the managerial structure in *every* organization.

To train supervisors, we need to know what they do and what they should be doing. Specific needs analysis can answer these points. In addition, external research shows some interesting themes which can be tested and made transferable to training in your organization.

A survey of first level managers (termed foremen in some industries, such as the steel industry, where part of this survey was conducted) showed some common tasks, different tasks, highlighted problems and seemed to suggest a 'contingency' approach to their job.[5] In more detail they were:

Common tasks Most of the managers performed similar types of duties. There was a lot of emphasis on 'man-management' and keeping 'order' among their units. Given the industry, there was, as is to be expected, an emphasis on safety and accident prevention.

Uncommon tasks The production people were very much man-managers, while the maintenance managers were more involved in planning, sustaining standards and report writing.

Problems There was a vagueness about the extent of their authority and responsibility. Technical data, particularly about machines, troubled some, while others had difficulty in getting hold of information on collective union agreements. Contacts with other departments were also problematic, and relationships with people (subordinates and middle management) caused difficulties for some. In particular younger (more inexperienced) foremen had difficulties with the workgroup, while the lack of consultation and advice on policies from above left the foremen at a loss on many occasions.

Contingency In larger firms, specialists helped foremen particularly over staff resourcing and record keeping. The job was not made easier, though, as bureaucracy developed and it resulted in more reports and man-management disciplinary meetings and union discussions taking up their time.

Thurley and Hamblin's study in the production area also highlights useful 'common denominators' that can be included in supervisory first-level management training:[6]

- *Communication* is the most time-consuming task, particularly feeding information *up* the management hierarchy.
- *Planning* and *scheduling* are important.
- *Monitoring, checking* and *inspecting* the work of others and the machinery are also ongoing.
- On the job *training* of operatives is important.
- *Problem solving* to cope with unplanned emergencies/deviations from the schedule was critical.

Again, contingency factors were evident. Differences in the production system, previous learning/training and the predominant managerial style impacted on how these tasks were carried out. Clearly we need to take account of the contingency factors in each organization.[7]

We have deliberately not gone down the route of managerial competencies as we are trying to extrapolate common denominators from empirical studies in the area. Again, we have been job or task-oriented. The qualities of the manager need to taken into account and the training implications noted. (See table 7.1.)

Table 7.1 Training implications of management 'qualities'

Quality	Range	Possible application to supervisors (experienced, 2/3 years + in post)
Command of the basic facts	'What is going on around here?' Includes sources of information to developing 'own' network.	Many supervisors vague on this area in the studies. Need to develop factual knowledge base.
Relevant professional knowledge	Up to date with latest thinking and how well informed is the individual.	Seemed to know 'their' task but within limits. *May* be less important for supervisor who is staying put.
Sensitivity to events	A 'tuning in' process to events and people.	A lot of people-management was a constant and relations 'above' often problematic. Need to develop sensitivity.
Problem solving	Essentially decision making and judgement.	Not just a routine decision maker. Often on own when operation goes off at a tangent. Need for information/policies to aid process and process of decision making itself to be sharpened.
Social skills	People skills and communication.	This was a constant in the studies. Need to keep on top.
Emotional resilience	Coping mechanisms with stress/tension etc.	From the studies, the ambiguity over role/responsibility could be stress-inducing and they must be prepared for the non-routine. Need to develop these 'coping mechanisms'.

Table 7.1   (Cont.)

Quality	Range	Possible application to supervisors (experienced, 2/3 years + in post)
Responding purposefully to events	This is taking the initiative and being in 'control'.	The role is active rather than passive as events move quickly. How much scope is given from above for real initiative? More senior people need to work more closely.
Creativity	Essentially new slants/new ideas.	Again, scope may be limited for coming up with bright imaginative ideas. If they do, more senior managers need to take an active role and work more closely.
Mental agility	Speed of thought/quick response to situations.	This is important when facing new unscheduled problems. Need to develop this thought process, if possible.
Balanced learning habits	Relating theory to practice and balanced approach to new learning situations.	Perhaps over-pragmatic and equating theory with obscure academic pedantics. Need for theory/practice integration.
Self knowledge	Conscious of own feelings/behaviour attitudes influencing actions/decisions, etc.	Gives more objectivity to decision making. Develop in problem solving.

Source: 'Qualities' adapted from J. G. Burgoyne et al., *Self Development, Theory and Applications for Practitioners*.

Box 7.2   Some principles behind supervisory training

- Macro themes must be dovetailed into your training needs.
- The first line manager's job is complex and it may vary on daily basis, so themes and priorities must be identified and ask supervisors to conduct their own job and task analysis.
- The programme has got to be practical.
- There is value in external programmes and 'exposure' once the supervisor has built up learning confidence on internal programmes.
- Clearer, less ambiguous job roles may be a non-training solution.
- Senior and middle management have a key role in developing, and communicating with the supervisors.

This type of 'macro' needs analysis must be supplemented by a systematic approach to specific training needs in the organization. This cannot be done here, hence this approach is used on its own. The end result would be an off-the-job/on-the-job programme containing these general needs derived from the 'task' and 'qualities approach'. A brief programme is seen in appendix 7A. This section concludes by summarizing some guiding principles (see box 7.2.)

Industrial Relations Training

Industrial relations concern conflict and job/workplace regulation. Of all the aspects of people management it is probably the one that can 'break' the organization. Indeed industrial conflict is often a harbinger of wider socioeconomic conflicts which result in the overthrow of the State. Examples range from Russia in 1917 (February and October) to 1991 in the Eastern European bloc.

The manager's interest in industrial relations tends not to be that of a counter-revolutionary ploy, but it is clearly identified with the security needs of the organization:

> ... The principal aim of management is to conduct the business of the undertaking successfully. Good industrial relations need to be developed within the framework of an efficient organisation and they will in turn help management to achieve this aim.

... Good industrial relations are the joint responsibility of management and of employees and trade unions representing them. But the primary responsibility for their promotion rests with management. It should therefore take the initiative in creating and developing them. (*HMSO, Industrial Relations Code of Practice.*)

So the code was really advocating a pro-active vision whereby management looked to 'positive' industrial relations to 'make' the organization. Hence industrial relations are an important function, and as such, training implications follow. Brewster and Connock defined the subject as:

Industrial Relations training is the systematic development of those involved with employment relationships so that such relationships may be handled more effectively. (C. Brewster and S. Connock, *Industrial Relations Training for Managers.*)

Many of our human and industrial relations difficulties can be levelled at a lack of coherent understanding, particularly by management, of an industrial relations philosophy, the absence of industrial relations policies and procedures and a negative approach to the subject which is seen as short-term 'problems' which disrupt the production flow. Training must be seen in perspective of establishing this 'effective' climate in the workplace. (See box 7.3.)

The manifestations of industrial relations training needs can be seen in examples of what management would deem to be 'poor industrial relations': high incidence of strikes, stoppages, go-slows and overtime bans; high level of absence and disciplinary issues; 'restrictive practices' inhibiting flexibility; poor productivity and poor customer relations; high labour turnover. Other pressures need to be taken into account: control, security, government, legal obligations, as well as the level of trust/conflict or the overall industrial relations 'climate' of the organization. It is an error to see industrial relations only as a problem.[8] Assuming we can widen this problem – orientation of industrial relations, benefits can accrue from industrial relations training. (See box 7.4.)

So assuming a training need, who should be trained and in what? We should focus on the worker and managerial hierarchies of the actors in the industrial relations system[9] and exclude governmental and private agencies as they are outside of the organization's training responsibilities.

Box 7.3 Establishing and maintaining effective industrial relations

---

- Nature of industrial relations and critical impact on the organization to be understood by all managers.
- Senior management must take ultimate responsibility for industrial relations and not just see these relationships as 'problems'.
- Line and staff managers to work closely together.
- A working 'frame of reference' which does not inhibit relationships is required, e.g. pluralist vision.
- Managers, trade unionists and all employees to be aware of their respective roles and responsibilities in industrial relations.
- Training is not necessarily *the* panacea for troubled relationships between management and organized labour.
- Other solutions (non-training) such as terms and conditions to be examined.
- There is a strong case for a written industrial relations policy and procedural guidelines for relationships at work.
- Above all else, it requires thorough understanding of the dynamics of industrial relations and a toleration of the 'opposition' and its point of view. The legitimacy of the other's role and activity must be recognized for industrial relations to get off the starting blocks.

Box 7.4 The advantages of industrial relations training

Developing: Skills, knowledge and attitudes necessary (to carry out policies, procedures and agreements).

Preparing: For changes.

Reducing: Problems attributed to human relations.

Linking: Planned improvements in the firm to national developments.

Source: Adapted from Distribution Industry Training Board, Recommendations on Industrial Relations Training.

The roles determine training needs. Here we discuss the roles, and the training implications are listed in appendix 7B.

The industrial relations roles are as follows:

Owner/directors/senior managers – Create and are accountable for the industrial relations policy and impact heavily on the climate of harmony or conflict.

Middle managers (line) – Maintain and develop policies and contribute to reformulation of new policies, operate procedures and are involved in face-to-face communications.

Staff managers (personnel) – Advisers to line and give specialist inputs in law as well as payment systems etc.

First line managers – They interact with the 'worker hierarchy' on a daily basis.

Senior shop stewards/convenors – A representative role for both the collective and individual interests of the trade union membership. May have 'company-wide responsibility'.

Employee representatives/shop stewards – A representative again, but for a smaller workgroup.

Employees – They are responsible for working within the agreed policies, procedures and agreements.

An alternative approach for *managers* has been used by Jennings and Undy writing in 1984.[10] Eight key industrial relations activities of managers can be highlighted in their research:

1 Dealing with trade unions.
2 Application of terms and conditions of employment.
3 Communication and consultation implementation.
4 Work organization and allocation.
5 Grievance handling.
6 Discipline and dismissal.
7 Health and safety implementation.
8 Equal opportunity implementation.

This may lack a context compared to the other approach but it gives a nitty-gritty grasp of the subject for training for one group of 'actors'. Another broader approach is to examine the nature of industrial relations and its subject matter which should be transferable to a training milieu.

Various approaches to the subject can be considered. The 'input/ output' approach sees industrial relations about converting conflict into some land of regulation. These conflicts of right or interest are seen to be reconciled through some institutions, or mechanism, such as collective bargaining. The input/output approach needs to be widened to take account of the environment. Dunlop's approach is highlighted in figure 7.1 below.

Figure 7.1 Industrial relations systems

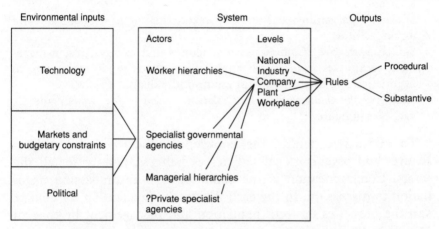

Source: Adapted from J. T. Dunlop, *Industrial Relations Systems*.

Of course this had been modified with time and the central issue of the system may be seen as the outputs (i.e. the rules) or the process of getting to these outputs.[11] The role of ideology and power could well be emphasized while other environmental influences such as social factors seem to be 'shelved'. Outputs assume rules and custom/practice and 'laws' need to be added while the scope for disagreement and conflict is not addressed in the output phase.

The actors' perceptions and definitions of what they see as 'real' (social action) is another perspective which begins to look more at ideas and the potential for conflicting ideas on the whole subject.

This gives us various perspectives and the weighting of the factors clearly differs according to the three approaches. The training aspects can be summarized as follows:

Environment Political, economic, social, legal and technological factors impacting on the firm need to be understood, as they form a base to national industrial relations and to the internal system of the organization.
The parties This would include philosophy, structure and roles of the main parties.
Goals Conflict, power and ideologies to be covered.

Relationships   Day-to-day interpersonal relations and inter/intra group relations and goal satisfaction or 'satisficing'.

Procedures and agreements   Discipline, grievance, dismissal, redundancy, negotiation and consultation.

Legal processes   Health and safety to equal opportunity to conciliation/arbitration.

Structure   Bargaining/consultation, negotiation units, recognition and union facilities.

Skills/competencies   Communication, money and pay systems, management techniques from organization and methods to job evaluation, to negotiation and interacting with groups/individuals.

Managing the changing industrial relations system – See system and its variables in figure 7.1.

To summarize, within the knowledge area, we find law, procedures and organizational policies as being important for all the actors. Communication is the common skill encompassing negotiation to discussion. In the early 1990s, the preparation for change and the pressures on joint regulation and management by consent seemed to be key issues in managing change. This 'change management' is discussed in the next section.

Managing Change: A Behavioural Approach to Training

Understanding 'change management'

External environmental conditions seem to be forcing the pace of organizational change. Political, technological, economic and market factors allied to rising social expectations, from the customer to the employee, emphasize this change. There has always been change but the difference lies in its pace and its degree. The 'turbulence' of the external environment has increased considerably since the mid 1970s.[12]

The analogy can be made between the animal in its natural habitat, adopting and adapting to its environment for its very survival, and the organization reacting to external environmental stimuli. Of course, all organizational change is not purely reactive. It has been proposed that change has an evolutionary form, emanating as much from *within* the organization as from *without*.[13] This evolutionary phased approach follows a natural ageing pattern not dissimilar to a product moving through its life cycle. A crisis, internal or external, moves the organization to the next phase of its natural development. Much of the literature and research on change management is concerned with understanding these pressures for change and for having a planned response to these developments.[14]

Training and change management

Training is a useful mechanism of change management. It is not the only tool, of course, but it has a role to play in at least three areas:

1 A technique to meet these planned changes.
2 Training can learn from the method of change management, particularly the problem-solving approach.
3 Training can assist in determining the degree to which a change may become permanent.

The range of managerial strategies, including training, to provide a basis for change is well documented in the literature.[15]

The 'interventions', so called because people are purposively becoming involved in this planned change, can be divided into:

- *techno-structural* approaches aimed at changing the technological variables that influence behaviour; and
- *process* approaches aimed at changing people's attitudes, value systems, norms of behaviour and task goals. This affects relationship within and between individuals and groups.

The techno-structural interventions are wider than training. Job enrichment experiments in giving greater workgroup autonomy and the application of contingency theories to the organization, all seem to predominate. There may be a role for training in getting these concepts and experiments more widely understood which may stimulate greater acceptance, but they are not really 'training types' of intervention.

The process techniques[16] have a distinct training 'feel' to them. Team building and development is a good example. The aim is to determine the effectiveness of a group. This covers the task in hand related to work procedures and the interpersonal relationships or the 'dynamics' or workings or the group. Leadership, formally assigned by the organization and informally assigned by the group, is an intrinsic part of this process. Group methods of problem solving, goal setting, communication and conflict resolution can be identified and altered through such 'interventions'. A third party, external facilitator, often acts as the agent for the group to build up its team identity. Work-related issues dominate and the group is usually made up of a section or unit of a department.

In part, related to this team building can be 'laboratory training'. The aim is to increase individual, if not group, sensitivity. The individual's behaviour, the behaviour of others, and the impact of both behaviours are analysed in a non-directive fashion. Again the tutor is a facilitator (experienced) who guides rather than instructs. Frank communication between the group members is encouraged and other group members give feedback on individual performance within this setting.

Intergroup sessions

We all tend to have a departmental or functional expertise which can lead to a blinkered approach to the organization-wide objectives. Conflicts arise between sections and departments, such as marketing and production. The intergroup sessions get the conflicting sections together. Again, self (group level) analysis of how one group perceives the way the other group thinks about it, a discussion on perceptions and a joint session on problem solving between the two groups are used to effect.

The grid etc.

This third stage is more organization bound. It may involve an application of the *grid* (Phases 1–6) and of *Likert's systems* approaches.[17] The *survey feedback* method is a useful technique for generating change and for highlighting potential discrepancies between organizational policies and practice. A broad survey of attitudes and views is taken and the answers collated and fed back to the workgroup. So this survey clears the ground, although positive action must follow later to blend fact and perception together.

Normative analysis

The main premise underlying this approach is that human behavioural change (learning) is best carried out by changing the culture, or the 'socio-corporate' environment within which that behaviour exists. The organization is evaluated, the desired norms established and the existing norms derived from surveys etc. The 'norm gap' thus exposed is closed to give the desired norms in which behaviour is found.[18]

So, the group dynamics, the intergroup sessions and the grid can make for more effective teamwork, which is also a concern of training – for training is not based just on the individual. The survey feedback and later stages of the grid can be linked to confrontational meetings in a developmental programme. Clarification of roles and the emphasis on goals can be useful techniques at the beginning of learning programmes. On technique, there is a link at the group level to managing change and training but this link becomes more tenuous at organizational level with norms and efforts to change the whole personality of the organization.

Training and change management methods

The line trainer can derive some benefit from the problem-based approach of the so-called 'change agents' and he or she can find some value in examining the roles of these 'agents'. The structured approach to problem solving may seem an indulgence to the over-stretched line manager/trainer but it has merit, for example: a 'live' research on problem identification; a diagnosis through applied research; solutions and alternatives derived from the research. It is particularly useful for training needs analysis but it makes for better decision making in non-training duties as well.

The role types of the change agent can equate to those of the staff trainer and may also be relevant to the line trainer. For example, the *expert* may be there to give or to sell expertise, irrespective of the real needs of the line manager. As the line trainer is not an 'expert' in this sense, the real needs of the department/section will not be overlooked. The ojective analysis does not really need the outside expert, as this book has tried to demonstrate. The line trainer, particularly at induction and on-the-job instruction may follow the route of the *teacher* with a focus on the individual trainee. Again a knowledge of this role should prevent 'courses for horses' being sprung on the line trainer from others.

The *counsellor* role, although time-consuming and exhausting, can act as a 'mirror' to subordinates. It is a hands-off approach to problem solving and requires a reflective frame of mind from the line trainer. It can also be an infuriating role to overstructured subordinates who expect an 'expert' decision from their manager. Hence it will be difficult to have an authoritarian-cum-expert approach for normal line management and wear the counsellor's hat for line training. So, the line trainer can learn more about what to expect from staff and consulting specialists and his or her own preferred role in dealing with problems, by analysing these problem-solving methods and diverse roles.

Training, change management and permanence

Both training and change management seek behavioural modification to increase individual and organizational effectiveness. So what can training learn from the permanence of these behavioural changes from the 'change agents'?

The pitch of involvement tends to be at the organizational and group levels in the management of change, while it tends to be at the individual, and to some extent group, level for training. However, if it works at the wider level it should work at the smaller level of training. A list of 'principles' has been gleaned from the research on change management which does have an influence on training management.

Principles of effective behavioural change

- Planning and a systematic diagnosis of problems are necessary.
- It must be top-led with sponsorship and commitment from senior management.
- There needs to be a degree of pressure to change (internal or external).
- It flourishes in an atmosphere of trust and co-operation and is more difficult in power-conflict situations.
- The 'change person' needs developed diagnostic skills.
- Links must be maintained to contacts inside and outside of the 'system'.
- A model or operational plan to guide changes is useful.
- The changes have got to be seen as non-threatening and helpful to all involved.
- There should be no blame placing on past failings.
- 'Ownership' of the change needs to be established with the employees.
- Timing is important and the pace needs to maintain a steady momentum over time.
- People need to know what is expected of them as a result of the change.
- Managers should seek commitment through employee involvement in the decision to change.
- Group pressures need to be accounted for as they can accept and sanction the change.
- Line management involvement and support is critical.

So behavioural changes at these levels have some useful lessons for line trainers, and some of these themes will be developed in the next chapter on evaluation and gaining/holding commitment for training.

Appendix 7A   Supervisor training

The programme for supervisor training will be divided into three aspects:

1 Self-development.
2 Routine aspects of management.
3 Non-routine aspects of management.

General guidelines follow.

Self-development

Analysis of the job to occur. Use of a diary method to track daily, if not hourly, tasks, contacts with people and types of issues problems encountered, etc. as the job is so varied, over a period of two weeks. This should include: task, duration, contacts, conclusion, etc. Critical incidents/ problems to be given more weight than any 'routine' tasks. If not evident, note *previous* critical/non-routine incidents where supervisors had to make a decision without consulting other more senior managers.

Once the 'job' is covered, the focus should be on the *individual*. Self analysis to be carried out using structured questionnaires and identification of perceived strengths and weaknesses. These strengths/weaknesses must relate to the job. 'Profile' of strengths/weaknesses derived from this self-assessment. Emotional resilience, for example, must be assessed. [Need for manager/specialist in profiling/psychometric testing to be on hand if a professional approach is to to be taken.]

Consideration of external educational programmes, e.g. CMS (Certificate of Management Studies), DMS, BTEC National or Higher in Business and Finance, if relevant to individual's age/career expectations etc.

Routine

Some of the job is 'routine' with almost a programmed element to it. For example, planning is short-term scheduling, control tends to be monitoring checking and quality assurance/control, organizing tends to be implementing of action planning backed up by policies and procedures of the organization. Reports/feedback on same.

The method of training will be two-fold:

1 On the job examining of existing controls, schedules and activity lists.
2 Off the job sessions on policies, procedures, control mechanisms and 'checks' as well as exposure to planning (including financial/costing implications) of projects. Report writing practice etc. to be built in.

Non-routine

The focus here is on the principles/practice of management, problem solving, team-work and people management/motivating staff. Employee selections and discipline/grievance, negotiations, etc. to be included as appropriate. The role as line trainer to be covered.

This is best handled in a structured format (three or four days) off-the-job seminars with 'real' cases and scenarios derived from the organization or industry.

Appendix 7B   Possible industrial relations training needs derived from roles[19]

Owners/directors/senior managers

- Sound understanding of 'macro' context of organization and impact on firm.
- Understanding of interface between union/company, e.g. full-time officials' roles, participation levels/machinery, etc.
- Sound understanding of industrial relations policies and procedures.
- Negotiation/consultation skills.
- Awareness of causes/nature of conflict and co-operation.

Middle managers (line)

- Awareness of macro context.
- Full understanding of policy and respective role.
- Working knowledge of union government and participation.
- Negotiation/consultation skills.
- Awareness of causes/nature of conflict and co-operation.

Staff managers

- 'Global' understanding of company industrial relations system.
- Sound knowledge of law, pay systems, manpower planning, etc.
- Specific role in disputes, grievances and negotiation of agreements.
- Research (labour) skills.

- Negotiation/consultation.
- Awareness of causes/nature of conflict and co-operation.

First level managers

- Detailed knowledge of policies, procedures and specific agreements.
- Detailed knowledge of role/responsibility in these procedures.
- Awareness of trade union rules and responsibilities of their officials (lay).
- Acceptance of importance of a fair and reasonable approach to human relations within the section/department.
- Knowledge of the ramifications of action/inaction on other sections.

Senior shop stewards/convenors

- Sound knowledge of union policies, rules and internal 'government' and of joint agreements, company policies etc.
- Liaison role with full-time official(s) and members.
- Representational/leadership role to the district/geographical area of the union and assisting in formulation of motions to conference.
- Good knowledge of labour law (individual and collective).
- Negotiation skills.

Shop steward

- Sound knowledge of company policies, joint agreements and overall union policies/rules.
- Good understanding of local industrial relations system.
- Awareness of own role and parameters.
- Understanding of role of others acting in the system.
- Negotiation and communication skills.

Employees

- Company rules to be learnt and understood.
- Union rights/obligations to be learnt and understood.
- Awareness of discipline/grievance machinery.
- Active membership of the union and the organization to be encouraged.

Notes

1 The learning of the culture of the subsociety (an organization) is social-ization. The accepted ways of doing things, the rules, the mannerisms, the dress code, guidelines of conduct and the norms, can be 'installed'

and reinforced at this initial session between individual and organization.

2 The concept of the 'informal organization' is well documented and is often seen as part of the organizational iceberg below the formal surface. The work of D. R. Roy is particularly helpful in showing norms of expectation and culturalization from the workgroup to the newcomer. See, for example, 'Banana time: Job satisfaction and informal interaction'.

3 See T. J. Peters and R. H. Waterman (Jnr), *In Search of Excellence: Lessons from America's Best Run Companies*. Their 'core' or 'shared' values go to the hub of the framework which includes strategy, structure, systems, style, staff and skills.

4 The debate on the effective organization is beyond the remit of this book, but certain norms would seem to facilitate effectiveness and induction training can get the individual off to a good start.

S. P. Robbins, in *Organisational Theory: Structure, Design, and Applications*, argues that there are eight effectiveness 'cells': (1) flexibility – the ability to adjust to shifts in external demands; (2) acquisition of resources – the ability to increase external resources; (3) planning – well-established goals; (4) high production and efficiency; (5) strong channels of information; (6) stability, or a sense of order; (7) cohesive workforce, and (8) a trained skilled workforce with the capacity (and, I would add, the willingness) to do their work properly.

The ethos of the organization can be cemented during this key period. Of course, the informal organization, with a counter ethos, may always be present.

5 P. B. Warr and M. W. Bird, *Identifying supervisory training needs*.

6 K. E. Thurley and A. C. Hamblin, *The Supervisor and His Job*.

7 The weightings and importance of these contingency variables will differ according to organization. C. Handy, *Understanding Organisations*, provides a listing of the main variables which are coming into play within the organization which facilitates analysis:

- *organization* – systems and structures; type of people; group relations; unions; leadership; history; objectives; size; values;
- the roles, ability and motivation of *individuals* to work;
- the economic, physical and technological *environment*, and perhaps he should have added political and social factors in the environment as well.

8 The research of J. T. Winkler, 'The ghost at the bargaining table: directors and industrial relations', notes that *if* senior line managers even contemplated industrial relations, and it seemed to be a big 'if', their vision was that industrial relations equate to *a* problem.

9 These terms and structures were used by J. T. Dunlop. He is recognized

by most as the 'father' of industrial relations theory as he codified the subject in the late 1950s and forwarded the 'system' as a mechanism of understanding the diverse subject. See J. T. Dunlop, *Industrial Relations Systems.*

10 See S. Jennings and R. Undy, 'Auditing managers' IR training needs'. See also S. Jennings, W. E. J. McCarthy and R. Undy, *Managers and Industrial Relations: The Identification of Training Needs.*

11 Modifications appear, for example, in the work of S. J. Wood, A. Wagner, E. G. A. Armstrong, J. F. B. Goodman and J. E. Davis, 'The industrial relations system concept as a basis for theory in industrial relations'.

12 See H. I. Ansoff, *Strategic Management.*

13 L. E. Greiner, 'Evolution and revolution as organizations grow.' The five phases of growth are seen through: creativity, direction, delegation, co-ordination and, lastly, collaboration.

14 See for example L. Lovelady, 'The process of OD: A reformulated model of the change process', and S. Fox and D. Smith, 'Perspectives in organizational analysis and the management of change'. For a rather critical look at the whole research on change and organizational development, see also T. Stephenson, 'OD: A Critique'.

15 See J. P. Kotter and L. A. Schlesinger, 'Choosing Strategies for change'.

16 E. Schein, *Process Consultation.*

17 The 'grid' and Likert's systems can be seen in R. R. Blake and J. S. Mouton, *The Versatile Manager: A Grid Profile* and R. Likert, *New Patterns of Management.*

18 R. F. Allen and S. Pilnick of Scientific Resources Inc. have used this 'normative' analysis to alter group mores and organizational culture. See for example the later published work of S. Silverzweig and R. F. Allen, 'Changing the Corporate Culture'.

19 These needs have been derived and extrapolated from: the various industrial training boards (ITBs) that I have been involved with such as the ones for distribution (DITB) and printing and publishing (PPITB); the Labour Relations Agency's (N Ireland) *The Consultative Draft Code of Practice in IR Training*; and years of greying hair as a practitioner in industrial relations in various industries, as well as consultancy experience in others.

8

Evaluation and Audit

Objectives

- To distinguish between evaluation and validation.
- To link effectiveness with evaluation.
- To conduct an evaluation on goal outcomes (people and task).
- To conduct an evaluation on the processes of getting to these goals.
- To use evaluation as a method of gaining recognition and for the acceptance of training.
- To be aware of other methods for gaining such recognition/ acceptance.
- to conduct a full audit of the training system as a means of evaluation.

'Speak softly and you won't need a big stick . . .'
D. Krech et al. commenting on J. L. Freedman's,
'Long term behavioural effects of cognitive dissonance',
Elements of Psychology.

Overview

To justify its existence training must be cost effective: the pay-off must be related to the costs involved.[1] The evaluation process is really a measure of this effectiveness. The early models of training had evaluation as the last stage of the four phases: needs, design, implementation *then* evaluation. Increasingly, *some* evaluation is now being seen as an integral part of each *phase*. For example, if the evaluation of the needs analysis dictated that a planned direction was mistaken there would be a knock-on effect to the design phase, etc. So there is an argument for a more fluid cycle rather than a purely mechanistic clockwork rotation. However, it is felt that the main crux of evaluation should be centred after the implementation phase, although we should not neglect the whole system.

Effectiveness through some evaluation is not the only basis for justifying training. There has to be a conscious policy of selling, marketing and manipulating the power structure as well as a professional approach to training to ensure commitment to this critical function.

Evaluation

Evaluation means determining the value of something. In turn, value means worth or usefulness. This can be seen in intrinsic terms of value 'within something', for example, the beauty of the Mona Lisa, as well as in utility terms of having a beautiful painting adorn a room; and it can be seen in financial terms with the work of art being seen as a priceless painting. Clearly there are degrees of value – intrinsic merit, utility/usefulness and some financial benefit *vis à vis* costs and the potential or actual benefit accrued.

Training, Evaluation and Validation

The assessment of the value of training is termed evaluation. Some years ago, the Department of Employment differentiated it from validation, a form of ratification:

> ... The assessment of the total value of a training system, course or programme in social as well as financial terms. E differs from validation in that it attempts to measure the ov benefit of the course or programme and not just the achie its laid down objectives. (Department of Employment, (
> *Training Terms.*)

Hence the emphasis in evaluation is on value; the er validation is meeting specific objectives. Validation is na related to evaluation and forms an integral step in the e' of evaluation. Again, from the definition, it is important to grasp the potential scale of evaluation from specific projects to the whole of the training system. Evaluation has also been equated to effectiveness. Training evaluation really equates to determining the effectiveness of the training event. The four stage method facilitates such an analysis of evaluation/effectiveness:

1 *Reaction* The response by the learner.
2 *Learning* The principles, facts, techniques, etc. that were learned.
3 *Job behaviour* Actual behaviour/job change at the place of work.
4 *Results* The tangible benefits from quality and quantity to reduced costs, etc.[2]

I believe that effectiveness goes to the core of evaluation. There are many approaches to effectiveness that we can translate for our purposes – see table 8.1.

Clearly some end results must be evident to justify the training. The key constituency approach is a political ploy playing to the 'paymaster' or 'master' whether it is the senior manager or the learner. The competency constituencies do not seem to hold water in our context. The systems view as presented here gives a refreshing insight into the means or the processes – but the ends should not be ignored. Throughout this book we have been looking at a professional way of meeting these processes within the system and this professional approach may also provide some criteria in terms of training which will help in evaluation. Hence effective evaluation must take account of both the ends and the means, although the ends prevail and this is the format used here.

So, we need to examine:

1 The outcomes, essentially in terms of performance or of meeting the 'training gap' so far as the organization is concerned.
2 The outcomes, to a lesser extent, for the individual's achievements and for meeting the aspirations of the learners.

Both these would be covered under the term 'validation'.

3 The process of getting there, the mechanics of the system would mean some evaluation.
  (a) in terms of the final outcome
  (b) in their own professional training terms.
4 The training system as a *whole* and not just specific interventions or programmes need some evaluation as well.

These would be a wider view of evaluation.

Table 8.1   Four types of effectiveness for training evaluation

View	Measure of effectiveness	Training implication
'Goal attainment'	Appraise in terms of accomplishments or ends being met. The ends to which the function was created to achieve are the key factors.	Is training purely to increase performance/profit/ efficiency? Does it not have some individual objectives as well, e.g. job satisfaction.
'Strategic constituencies'	The environmental demands that impact on the very survival of the function are critical, hence these 'threats' must be appeased as the effectiveness test.	Is there some governmental pressure that we must appease? There was at one time in the UK, and possibly we had training for the ITB's benefit owing to the money involved. Without external pressures, senior managers, with the purse-strings, are the key constituency.
'Competing constituencies'	Criteria being used depends upon who you are, a trade union or a training manager. Hence 'no best way'.	Shows diverse preferences and could degenerate into diverse shopping lists.
'Systems'	The weight should be on inputs, processing these inputs channelling these inputs and transforming them to outputs. So resource acquisition, maintenance and successful interaction are important.	This is in line with the sub-parts identified in the text which are all interrelated and make up the whole of the system.

Source: The four 'views' are adapted from S. P. Robbins, *Organisational Theory*.

For the operational line trainer (and for the operational staff trainer) the main weight of the evaluation will be on goal outcomes (No. 1) and to a lesser extent the people goals (No. 2) and, of course, the process of getting there (No. 3) is integral to the whole system of training from needs to design to implementation. The system (No. 4) as a whole and its environmental interface is the evaluative role of more strategic managers, and as such we will mention it, but the focus is on operational issues.

To summarize, the goals or ends must be examined and so must the processes or means of meeting these ends. The overall system is seen as contextual for our evaluative purpose. One other variable seems to be present: is the evaluation directed at the needs/aspirations of the organization or individual/learner? A sample of approaches has been taken which illustrates these three dimensions of: focus (goals/process); direction (organization/learner); and level or scope (individual programme/training cycle/whole training system). See table 8.2 for a summary.

We should look at each of their main approaches on their own merit as they may satisfy your requirements. Again, of course, the methods and techniques of doing the evaluation are linked to the approach.

A process approach to organizational needs based on a whole system

Morris usefully widens the debate on evaluation by taking a more global approach.[3] Each part of the process or activity must be evaluated in this system which encompasses the external organizational environment down to the minutae of group and departmental change (see appendix 8A). Training evaluation is seen as 'highly analogous to problem-solving and decision-making approaches'. That is, a decision-cum-problem-solving technique with a decision type of tree is used by Morris. This may well be the case, but the issue is based on the degree of learning rather than the degree of decision making. These points apart, the checklist is quite useful.

1. *The macro context* This covers the outside world and business priorities and objectives. However, the external influences are one way only, impacting on the organization and are mainly informational-cum-market intelligence derivations. This is too narrow a focus. Again, it would be useful to have an evaluative

Table 8.2   Evaluation: A range of approaches

	Morris[a]	*Hamblin*[b]	*Quantified*	*Qualified*	*Donnelly*
Focus					
Goals		√	√	√	
Process	√				√
Main direction					
Organization needs	√	√	√		√
Learner needs				√	
Shared needs					
Level/scope of evaluation					
Individual programme or initiative		√	√	√	
Training cycle	included in system		√		√
Whole training system (incl. environment)	√	√			

[a] M. Morris, 'The evaluation of training'
[b] A. C. Hamblin, *Evaluation and Control of Training*

'norm' from outside the organization as Morris is too organization bound. For example, money spent on each apprentice or the number of under-twenty-ones attending day release, etc. would help this assessment. This could be norms for the industry or indeed international comparisons. This would be monitoring from a State-sponsored agency or revamped ITB or TEC.

Business/Training Interface   In essence the unstated aspect of this evaluation process seems to be the political/professional clout of the trainers. This political-cum-professional contribution is lacking in this model but we develop it later.

Training policies   Relationships between organizational and training objectives are to be clarified, according to Morris. This is seen as critical. However, the individual/personal needs are a little neglected.

Programme preparation Needs analysis, setting objectives, design and resource, constraints/opportunities add to the fine-tuning of the evaluative process. However, there is a lack of criteria to evaluate these aspects of the process.

Pre-Course activity This is useful for courses (and other programmes?) and is essentially informational dissemination to delegate to determine whether we have conscripts or volunteers!

Training activity This covers activity, reaction and learning and has been covered in previous approaches.

Behavioural change This is the mainstream approach that we will examine later.

Altogether a useful systems approach that escapes from the nitty-gritty activities of others. Yet criteria problems must be faced in this contextual analysis. We will return to potential techniques/methods of doing this evaluation – although Morris does not take this step in his approach.

A goal approach to organizational needs based on individual programmes or initiatives

This is a classical nitty-gritty approach and the work of Hamblin can be cited as a good example.[4] This goes to the heart of most of the approaches to the evaluation of training. It is based on a cause and effect approach. Essentially there is a level of 'objectives' (five in all) which impact on five 'effects', and in turn these impact on the initial five 'objectives'. Hence the effect becomes an ingredient of the new level of causation. (See figure 8.1.)

With the exception of the *ultimate value* objectives/effects, a leading nationalized UK Industry seems to have adopted Hamblin's cycle as part of its 'table of evaluation levels'.

The *reaction level* occurs at the end of the session and later after a short period 'on the job'. It is carried out by questionnaires, syndicate interview or discussion. The next stage, the *learning level* occurs not only at the end of the session, but it is ongoing throughout the

Figure 8.1   Hamblin's evaluation process

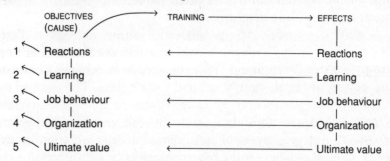

Source: Derived from A. Hamblin, *Evaluation and Control of Training*

formal training. Use is made of tests, both written and practical, and critique sessions occur.

The next level of *job behaviour* seems to be slightly more difficult to quantify. It occurs in the initial period of operational work and some three to six months after the event. The methods include: observation, self-assessment, questionnaires, interview and performance appraisal.

Organizational level, the next phase, relates to the achievement of organizational objectives via training. This is deemed to occur when performance is influenced by training. The method seems to centre on research into organizational effectiveness. Without reopening this debate on training/effectiveness of the organization (see chapter 1) the links are tenuous at best while training/non-training influences are difficult to isolate, and quantification seems even more remote.

Ultimate value is the apex. It seems to be almost metaphysical – unless the intrinsic value of training is seen at individual level – rather than the organizational level. Even then, if this was the case, it would be difficult to gauge and impossible to justify in most commercial organizations.

Quantification

This is a goal-oriented approach operating for organizational benefit at the level of individual performance. As seen with Hamblin's objectives, it is a lot easier to evaluate lower down the scale at the 'reaction' and 'learning' levels. These levels tend to answer the validation question: 'were the training objectives achieved?'

The *costs approach* is related to this validation level. The budget as a form of managerial control is often evident in training departments and in most line departments.

It is feasible to work out budgets with due costs, and variance analysis for training centres covering administration, lighting/heating, building/accommodation, meals/drinks, hotels, refreshments, course material, equipment and tutor's time. The costs of the trainees' time off the job can be gauged from their wage/salary rate. It is far more difficult to budget for on-the-job activities under such headings. So we can determine the costs of off-the-job training and possibly have a stab at on-the-job training either by sharing fixed training costs/and allocating costs by time involved by manager/trainee. This would help departmental budgetary concerns but not training evaluation as we would have to ally costs to the benefits accrued.

Opportunity costs This builds on the basic budgetary concept by examining: 'what if we do more selection or pay more money, compared to pumping money into training?' This is best refuted from a training perspective by relating the issue to a training problem (assuming it is) and having specific learning objectives by programme which can be attained and measured, if not costed. This type of analysis would relate to an evaluation at the time of needs analysis in the overall system of training and would be involved in the training plan.

Cost effective measures Again this is a comparative analysis and it may be useful in examining one design method as opposed to another, or indeed one course at a business school or 'buying in' outside help for management development. It assumes a basic costing procedure is in operation. The levels of comparative effectiveness in meeting needs may be more difficult to establish, for presumably the objectives are met or not unless the learning objectives have gradations of importance and priority.

Cost-benefit measures Do the benefits outweigh the costs? However, priority of objectives may be difficult and longer time-scales may be required to get a 'feel' for the longer-term benefits.

These cost-benefit measures would particularly apply at the implementation phase, and indeed the run up costs of the whole training cycle for a given programme, needs analysis and design must be taken into account. The benefit side is going to be difficult to quantify in many training situations.

Given the market-led approach which is creeping into the public sector in the UK, we now find a desire for surplus or profit and not only 'breaking even' in some training departments with their tendering and 'charging out' policies to their own council. This feedback or clients coming back to them is not so much a positive evaluation of their work but more of an acceptability test that has been passed.

Human investment   If people are a resource, they may be also an investment.[5] Human asset accounting attempts to put a price tag on people and looks to added value from the 'raw material' stage to the 'finished product'. Training indeed gives such added value, but the 'added value' is also related to a host of behavioural factors from personality to peer-group pressure. Such human investment appraisal seems to be problematic at this time.

Table 8.3 gives a summary of the possible methods we could use in this quantified approach.

So once again we find the early phases easier to come to terms with than the more complex phases later on. The techniques available reflect this trend. Clearly quantification on its own is not the definitive answer. Anyway, some would argue that training is about people and their needs so we should attempt to make some evaluation of the people side of the people/task equation.

A goal-directed approach with an emphasis on learner needs in an individual programme or initiative

A 'softer' approach to the quantification route is to examine the views and attitudes of learners over time. Parlett takes more of a 'feelings' approach to counter the task orientation of other views.[6] The evaluation, according to Parlett, should focus on perceptions and opinions as well as the behaviour of 'tutor' and 'student'.

The *repertory grid* is one mechanism of this qualitative approach. This grid has been developed from a vision of personal constructs or 'mental maps'.[7] The map is divided into 'elements' and 'constructs'. 'Elements' are akin to more concrete factors such as the person; while the constructs are more qualitative aspects such as 'cold and aloof' etc. If the 'pre, during and after' approach is adopted the grid can be useful employed in attitudinal/social skills training and gives a feel for the individual trainee's changing priorities.

Table 8.3 Quantification – Methods of training evaluation

Type	Method	Comment
Costs	As per learning/reaction but with 'price tag', costings and variance analysis.	Some value.
Opportunity costs	Cost of training compared with doing nothing/or other interventions.	Useful – for back up to rationale for training.
Cost effective	Relative costs to objectives.	Feasible, but 'pricing' of objectives = ?
Cost benefit/profit	Benefits outweigh costs?	Difficult.
Human investment	Human asset accounting, value added schemes, etc.	Sounds great but . . .

The learner's views over time concerning learning must be in-built into any evaluative machinery. The learner's needs/wishes must be tallied with the objectives of the line/staff trainer. A view is taken on past performance, a time-scale given, and a more people-oriented Hamblin approach then comes to the surface.

The first stage is the *derived learning needs*. This gives a context, or indeed a benchmark, on what the training is attempting to achieve. These derived needs can be made apparent to the trainer (line/staff) and to the trainee – if they are not self evident at the outset. *Assumed learning* is the trainee's immediate post-programme views on what he or she has learned. *Learning transfer* is the actual bridge from learning on the programme to the impact on the job.

Table 8.4 gives a 'feel' for some of the possible techniques open to the evaluation of the learner-centred approach.

A process-centred approach, meeting organizational needs at the level of the training cycle

Donnelly suggested the need for evaluation indicators *with criteria* at every phase of the training cycle.[8]

There are four main 'blocks':

Table 8.4   The learner-centred approach and some possible methods of evaluation

Type/Level	Possible method	Comment
1 Derived learning needs	Appraisal, job analysis, job sampling etc.	Critical.
2 Assumed learning	Individual's perspectives may need tutor's view. 'Happiness sheets' or past course reaction sheets used.	Much evaluation takes place at this level. Some value if integrated with 1 + 3.
3 Actual learning	Tests (before/after), questionnaires to the individual trainee and to manager, attitude measurement and ratings of performance (before/ after programme).	Pre/past 'testing' useful. Recall may not be real learning though! Some use.
4 Learning transfer (to job)	Time-scale problems and 'interference', self-appraisal and appraisal by manager.	Some use if honest self-analysis and objective appraisal by the manager can help.

1 *Resource availability*   This covers budgets to policies. Evaluation criteria includes options and acceptability.
2 *Need assessment – organization*   This is from sequence of operation to statutory requirements. Evaluation criteria covers availability of objective's acceptability and potential evaluators.
3 *Need assessment – job*   This covers job descriptions to the cost of error. Performance criteria and target population form the evaluators.
4 *Design*   Behavioural objectives to on/off-job training is covered. Evaluation includes method, content and timing of evaluation, evaluators and use of evaluation material.

Donnelly lists pre-entry requirements in order to progress from one block to another. These cover span of assessment to cost-benefit potential.

This approach is a lot tighter than the previous 'process' model. The evaluator indices within and before each progressive step are useful criteria. It is 'light' on the people side and perhaps needs a broader sweep to encompass the wider system. Altogether though, it seems to be the most innovative and helpful to date.

So where are we? Well, the evaluation of training is not so easy as some commentators imply. The validation of training is easier: clear objectives, knowledge of the 'antecedents', 'transactions' and 'outcomes' can be zoomed into.[9] The role of the learner should not be ignored in this task oriented objectives vision to give relatively clear-minded views of the actual impact of training.[10] Clearly, the longer the time-scale after the event, the more variables come to the fore and the training strand is diluted. So it has to have a realistic time period to make it feasible – months rather than years. The evaluation of the overall training system is more difficult and we will come back to this area at the end when we suggest an 'audit'-type of approach. In the interim, the clear objectives, defined in behavioural terms with given levels of achievement to be reached can be appraised by a before, during and after type of validation. However, this in itself may not be sufficient to mobilize interest or funds for training within the organization and it is to this area that we must turn.

Getting and Maintaining Commitment for Training

This is approached from the line trainer's perspective. The tactics can be equally employed by the staff trainer, although the 'client' of course may differ. The senior management, particularly line managers, need to be satisfied that training is cost effective; the learner must be willing and able to be trained; and the training gospel must reach the line managers who can see themselves as line trainers as well as functional specialists, finance or whatever, or generalist managers. So in many ways the staff trainer's role in getting and maintaining commitment has a focus on both senior and middle line managers, while the line trainer has a vested interest in the focus of senior management. The learner's needs are constant to both.

The initial entry point in 'getting in' as well as 'maintaining it once you are in' can be looked at from four perspectives:

1 marketing
2 sales
3 power/political
4 professional training.

Marketing

This is the provision of goods and services that the customers really need or want. It is a customer/client-oriented approach as opposed to a pure production/sales viewpoint where goods are made and then 'sold' – perhaps with little real concern for what people actually want or need.

> ... Selling focuses on the needs of the seller; marketing on the needs of the buyer. Selling is preoccupied with the seller's need to convert his product into cash; marketing with the idea of satisfying the needs of the customer by means of the product ...   (T. Levitt, 'Marketing myopia'.)

Marketing is demand management. Need/wants identification, the anticipation of change and the provision of services to satisfy the client are the main phases of marketing. Such an approach in training, would focus on the needs of the management decision makers, who impact on training budgets, the 'release' of trainees and who generally have the facility to encourage training or otherwise. The learner's needs should also be evident. The managerial client is more of an industrial type of market, whereas the consumer type of market may characterize the learner's needs. Political clout lies with management, so we will pay them more attention.

The marketing mix of the four Ps – product, price, promotion and place – is a reasonable mechanism of seeking some transferability to training. Place is more geared to implementation strategy while price may be an accountancy convention between departments or a critical aspect of the cost benefit analysis as discussed earlier. Product and promotion are more important to our needs.

Product

Training is an intangible service and, as such, may be quite difficult to market. A strategy for marketing the concept must take account of: To whom is it directed? When? Where? What specific qualities are evident? Is the range adequate? Is it related to business need? The analysis derived from the training needs diagnosis may fulfil a marketing research requirement as well. The internal 'product range' must be geared to the changing business environment to have strategic credibility with top management. Innovation and new product development or training design is critical to this dynamic perspective.

Promotion (Excluding sales)

There has to be a coherent 'personality' coming over from the training department that managers can identify with. It has not to come over as a 'soft option', staffed by failed line managers, working in a training centre far removed from the coal-face.

Internal imagery can be reinforced by an external public relations (PR) image, from involvement with unemployed skill training to other State interventions in training. A high internal profile can be seen through conferences, guest speakers, receptions, workshops for line/staff trainers and handbooks indicating checklists for needs analysis etc.

Place

Although this is not seen as critical in this context, the 'determination of channels' may have significance. The line trainer needs the same motivation and co-operative attitude of a firm's agents or dealers. The agency idea, however, means being subordinate to the principal (the training department) and I prefer the full partnership analogy. The line trainer as an agent has some merit though if the level of agreement or sophistication inhibits a fuller partnership.

Price

Whether mark-up, full costing, or cost plus formulae are used, training has to have some break even analysis as a minimum, although internal competitive pricing akin to the external market, such as courses, seems less than relevant.

Buyer behaviour

The management (senior?) are seen as the 'buying unit'. Hence quantifiable benefits, rational argument and profitability through the value added that training brings, are key themes in 'selling' training. The buyer may be protective of the budget. Emphasis must be on the benefits and this is akin to 'industrial buying' and the buying 'grid'. (See appendix 8B.)

The straight re-buy is easiest, the modified re-buy means selling skills will be in demand, and the new task is to sell on virgin territory. The line and staff trainers would need to be in at the beginning of each of the eight buying phases (see appendix 8B) to market 'their' goods to their respective clients, senior management for line trainers or line management who have not yet become line trainers for the staff training specialist.

Buyer behaviour – the learner   The learner may be dragooned into learning, so choice and buyer behaviour may not be strictly transferable. Given that learner commitment and motivation may be the key to the acceptance of training, buyer behaviour may have more relevance than at first glance: the buyer may 'purchase' it or leave it alone.

The approach by Howard-Sheth majors on 'brand comprehension', 'satisfaction' and 'intention'.[11] A training manual/handbook allied to detailed discussions before a learning event gives 'brand comprehension'. 'Satisfaction' and 'intention' are allied to the learning situation, the design and the implementation of training. Satisfied customers make marketing easier but the trainer, line or staff, may still have to use persuasion.

Persuasion and Selling

We must assume that there is sufficient publicity and promotional literature on training to ease the sales effort. If not, time will be spent selling the concept rather than the practice of training. A sales approach communicates the advantages of the product/service to the client, manager or learner. In spite of marketing efforts, persuasion or selling may still need to prevail to outline the merits of the service and to demonstrate individual value to the client(s).

Some of the mechanics of sales technique must be noted to facilitate persuasion. First, the negative imagery of selling must be ironed out. The message must get over so information and persuasion are necessary.

'Buyer behaviour' must be understood by the line and staff trainer to gauge the right level or 'pitch'. 'Prospecting for customers' is relatively easy as the organization is a closed internal market. Data and personal information on the buyers abound within the organization.

The communication process of delivering the message is critical and 'closing the sale' terminology may not be too far removed from the training reality in many organizations. The final part of selling is maintaining good 'client relationship' after the event – and this is clearly transferable to training.

In themselves, marketing/selling may work, but the power structure within your organization can vitiate any such initiatives.

Politics

To gain entry and to sustain effort, we need to understand and use organizational politics. The ability to manipulate power systems may be critical for training.[12] This view of power is seen as:

> ... the capacity to modify the conduct of other employees in a desired manner, together with the capacity to avoid having one's own behaviour modified in undesired ways by other employees. (R. N. McMurray, 'Power and the ambitious executive'.)

Self benefit at the expense of others is another view.[13] For example, we are told not to cross our legs, but to plant our feet firmly on the ground to project an aura of solid power. Or, better still, speak low, to make others lean forward to hear what you have to say. Whilst not denying these approaches, power and its political undertones must be given a context in which the line and staff trainers operate.

Cliques tend to operate in most organizations. The classic work of Dalton showed the 'ins' and the 'outs'.[14] Masonic allegiance, Republican views and Anglo-Saxon descent made the individual a member of the 'ins'. Trainers need to be aware of the existence of powerful cliques, masonic or not, in their organization.

So, how can the line and staff trainer enhance their power? Some five distinct bases exist: reward, referent, legitimate, expert, and coercive.[15] The trainers, line and staff, will get little mileage out of coercive power, given what they are trying to do. Legitimate power is given by the organization and rested in the job (not holder). The power base of staff trainers often looks light; while the power of line trainers because they are in the direct line or chain of command is far heavier. Rewarding people for training, either senior management or learner, seems a little strange. Referent power with the subordinates identifying with the manager is particularly important for both line and staff trainers. Both trainers need expert power derived from a professional approach to training. When allied to legitimate power, a recipe for success looks possible.

Pettigrew, Jones and Reason give us a whole gambit of power bases for their range of trainer roles, as listed below.[16] Of course, these are geared to staff not line trainers.

> *'Borrowed' power* from external authorities, agencies or specialists. It can give more credence to an existing power base but is insufficient in itself.
>
> *Relationships* Being known for positive things and having a high profile in the organization can be linked to the old boys/girls network.
>
> *Ability* Being known for the good track record and technical competence all help the credibility aspect.
>
> *Policies* Training policies and procedures can be easily flouted and the trainer who attempts to use them to build up power may be perceived by others as hiding behind the papers/bureaucracy. They can help but are adjuncts only of real power.
>
> *Allies* Top level support and allies with the ear of the top decision makers can help.

Perhaps the line trainer does need to talk quietly and not attempt to wield a big stick. Organizational sensitivity and social graces coupled to good interpersonal skills and 'blending in' to the norms to the organization are all-important political skills.

Position power, a network and backing from the top help make the politician effective. The politics should be for the sake of training not self-aggrandisement, and a competent professional approach is critical to the whole acceptability of training.

Professional Training Skills and Knowledge

All the marketing, sales and political initiatives amount to mere ploys unless we have a sound professional base. We analysed these competencies and 'common cores' of the role earlier. To summarize:

- Both the line and staff trainer need 'direct training' skills from learning methods to techniques of input and instruction.
- The staff trainer must be a good administrator of the training system and the line trainer must be aware of this system, its resources and its requirements.
- 'Determining training' from environmental awareness to needs analysis and learning design is another key aspect.

- 'Consulting' or diagnostic approaches from counselling to coaching to listening to organizational and job analysis are equally important.

John Kenney, in 1976, highlighted core competencies of a staff trainer which can be applied equally to both the line and staff trainer:

- Learning theory.
- Communication.
- Administration.
- Person–organization interface.
- Process.
- Group dynamics.
- Manpower planning.
- Training needs analysis.
- Course design.
- Teaching practice.
- Training equipment/materials.
- Evaluation.[17]

So, marketing, sales, power-based and professional-cum-competency approaches to getting training recognized and established have been covered. Of course, they are not neat discrete boxes. At the end of the day the building block to entry and to ongoing relationships must be proven ability at training and being able to justify your actions and to point to success. This takes us back to validation and evaluation.

Validation has been covered and this was seen to be feasible. Evaluation proved more elusive. Consequently, as a conclusion to the book, and indeed to the whole system of training, we are going to look at an *audit* of training which acts as an evaluator of the training system, and feeds into the next 'inputs' and 'transformation processes' of the whole scheme of things.

The Training Audit

This training audit is based on the training system represented in this book. (See appendix 8C.)

The system of training used in this text was not only a structural device to hold the book together, but it was put forward as a working representation of everyday training reality in organizations. The checklist is based on this system, which will help to complete the audit, which in turn will act as an aid to evaluating the whole training system.

This checklist assists in auditing best theory and practice within training and so contributes to the overall evaluation of the training system. As it happens, the training system being proposed for consideration as a representation of organizational reality has also provided the framework for this book, so the checklist provides a useful summation of the text. Hence there will be no more summaries of the content, only a reiteration of the two main themes.

The literature of training has increasingly focused on:

1 The role of the learner and his or her style on a spectrum of participative learning.
2 The training department and the roles of the training specialists.

This book has given a new dimension.

1 Of course the learner is important but he or she must be placed in the context of the training system which is equally, if not more, important.
2 Apart from the learner, there must be a 'learning partnership' between the staff specialist trainer and the line manager responsible for people.

On a final note, this tale from the village where I live, highlighted by *The Cambridge Weekly News* (5 December 1991), puts the whole of the book into perspective.

> A gas works once existed in Station Road, Melbourn – just a stone's throw from the route of the old A10. There is a story that when the man who operated it died just before the First World War *no one else knew how it worked*. The village was forced to revert to oil lamps until the advent of electricity some ten years later.

Appendix 8A   Evaluation

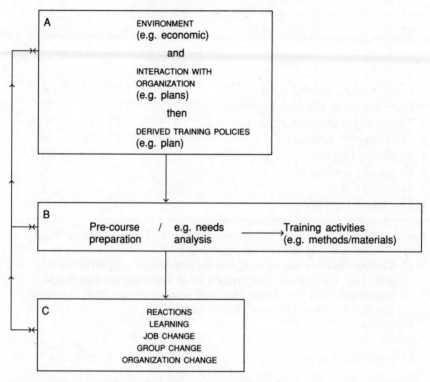

Note: Evaluation by training decision making and longer-term decision making (non-training) at each phase.

Source: Adapted from M. Morris, 'The evaluation of training'.

Appendix 8B   Buying behaviour

Behaviour	New task	Modified re-buy	Straight re-buy
1 Anticipating a general need	Y	?	N
2 Determining features and quantity	Y	?	N
3 Describing features and quantity	Y	Y	Y
4 Searching for 'sources'	Y	?	N
5 Analysing proposals	Y	?	N
6 Evaluating proposals	Y	?	N
7 Selecting orders	Y	?	N
8 Evaluating feedback	Y	Y	Y

Source: Adapted from Patrick J. Robinson, Charles W. Faris and Yoram Wind, *Industrial Buying and Creative Marketing*, p. 14.

Note: The most difficult buying scenarios are at the upper-left part of the 'buy grid'. Here the many decision makers combine with many variables to present this difficulty. Again, the initial phase of the new task, as always, presents the greatest difficulty for the line trainer.

Y = Yes, N = No, ? = ?

Appendix 8C   The Training Audit checklist – based on the Training System

Environmental interface

☐ Do you regularly 'scan' the external environment of your organization?

☐ Are you familiar with the main trends within your environment?

☐ Have you conducted a 'PEST' (political, economic, social and technological scan of the external environment) type of analysis?

☐ Are there any training implications from 'PEST'?

☐ What are your industry 'norms' on training?
 e.g. number of apprentices etc.

☐ Are there any urgent priorities emanating from your environment?
 e.g. quality standards/BS 5750 etc.

☐ Will proposed organizational changes impact on your environment?

☐ Do you have a corporate plan and a human resource plan?

☐ Are the training plan/priorities related to business/organizational need?

☐ How do the corporate plan/HR plan impact on training priorities?
 e.g. product launch etc.

Training need

☐ Is there a people problem?
☐ Is there a task or performance problem?
☐ Is it training? Have you looked at alternatives?
  e.g. money, selection etc.
☐ Have you conducted a needs analysis?
☐ Is the analysis pitched at the right level of 'intervention'? (i.e. department, individual, etc.)
☐ What techniques are you using to analyse the need? Are they consistent with the level of intervention?
☐ Is the method: (a) acceptable to potential trainees?
              (b) sound?
☐ Have you drawn up a plan of campaign with priorities?
☐ Can you cost the training?
☐ Outline the benefits that you expect.
☐ Can you cost these benefits?

Management

☐ Have you got commitment from the top?
☐ If not what strategy are you adopting?
  e.g. sales, politics, etc.
☐ Do you have an adequate budget?
☐ Is there a training plan, policy or guideline?
☐ Who does what?
☐ What is your training role?
☐ Are you clear about the role?
☐ Have you been trained in this role?
☐ Have you read the relevant section of this book on your role?

Learning

☐ Have you determined the learners' styles?
☐ Have you adapted the event/programme to these styles?
☐ Have you considered the background of the 'audience'? e.g. age, maturity, experience, prior knowledge, etc.
☐ What is their level of past training?
☐ Are the trainers competent at presentation and delivery?
☐ Have the trainers (line and staff) considered their own approach to learning and styles of learning?
☐ Where does their real competence/experience lie?
☐ Are they facilitators, or lecturers?
☐ Are the main learning characteristics known?
☐ Are these characteristics accepted by trainees and 'tutors'?

☐ Are these characteristics in-built to the design of the event?
☐ Can they be used for evaluation purposes?

Design

☐ Does the design relate to the needs?
☐ Are there specific objectives? If not, create them.
☐ Can you classify your objectives into behavioural terms?
☐ Can you quantify them?
☐ What methods are you using?
☐ Do you relate design to level/degree of student/trainee participation?
☐ Is practice critical?
☐ Is knowledge and understanding foremost?
☐ Can you classify your design activity into learning characteristics/ 'principles'?
☐ Are the overall objectives feasible?
☐ Is the design method related to need?
☐ Have you used *a* systematic procedure/process of training?

Implementation

☐ How does the implementation plan relate to organizational/departmental priority(ies)?
☐ Have you policy statements that can act as key guidelines?
☐ Do you have a dynamic plan covering the who, why, where, etc. of training?
☐ Have you met both internal and external pressures/needs?
☐ Can you mobilize the promised resources (physical, financial and personnel)?
☐ Do you have experienced line and staff trainers?
☐ Do you need external assistance?
☐ What tasks can best be handled on the job?
☐ Do you have coherent implementation programmes for both on and off-the-job training?
☐ What are the key priorities for the next 12 months that have to be met?

Evaluation

☐ Do you have 'feedback loops' in built in the whole training system?
☐ Do you conduct validation?
☐ Can your clear behavioural objectives be measured?
☐ Have you qualitative measures to gauge trainees' reactions?
☐ What criteria did you use?
☐ Have you attempted a cost/benefit analysis?
☐ Have you used this checklist to help you audit your training 'in its own terms'?

Notes

1 Managers need a price tag on things and perhaps we need to quantify the costs and benefits of the training wherever possible, once the audience has been 'hooked'. Perhaps, as Krech et al. note, attitudinal change has to be involved in the 'inner person' to be permanent rather than imposed from the outside. So conviction is important. See D. Krech, R. S. Crutchfield and N. Livson, *Elements of Psychology*, p. 769.

2 Adapted from B. Taylor and G. Lippitt, *Management Development and Training Handbook*.

3 M. Morris, 'The evaluation of training'.

4 A. C. T. Hamblin, *Evaluation and Control of Training*.

5 See J. Cannon, *Cost Effective Decisions*.

6 See M. Parlett 'Evaluating innovations in teaching.

7 The 'mental map' and constructs has been usefully employed by M. Smith, 'Using repertory grids to evaluate training'.

8 E. Donnelly, 'The training model: Time for a change?'.

9 R. E. Stake, 'The countenance of educational evaluation'.

10 M. Parlett, 'Evaluating Innovations in teaching'.

11 The Howard-Smith Marketing Model for buyers' decisions is quite insightful. See J. A. Howard and J. N. Sheth, *The Theory of Buyer Behaviour*.

12 See R. Christie and F. L. Gers (eds), *Studies in Machiavellianism*.

13 M. Korda, *Power! How to get it*.

14 M. Dalton, *Men who Manage*.

15 J. R. P. French and B. H. Raven 'The bases of social power'.

16 A. M. Pettigrew, G. R. Jones and P. W. Reason, *Training and Developmental Roles in their Organisational Setting*.

17 J. Kenney, 'Core competencies of a trainer'.

Bibliography

Allen, L. A., 'Improving line and staff relationships', in *Studies in Personnel Policy*, No. 153, National Industrial Conference Board, New York, 1956.

Althusser, L., *Lenin and Philosophy and Other Essays*, New Left Books, London, 1977.

Anderson, A. and Tobbell, G., *Costing Training Centres*, IMS Report, No. 72, Institute of Manpower Studies, Brighton, 1983.

Anderson, A. H., 'Training and learning', in *Managing Human Resources*, 2nd edn, eds A. G. Cowling and C. J. B. Mailer, Arnold, London, 1990.

Anderson, R. H., 'Selection of media: Another perspective', *Improving Human Performance*, 3 (3), 1974.

Annett, J., *Skill Loss*, Manpower Services Commission, Sheffield, 1983.

Annett, J., Duncan, K. D., Stammers, R. B. and Gray, M. J., *Task Analysis*, Info. Paper, No. 6. HMSO, London, 1979.

Annett, J. and Sparrow, J., *Transfer of Learning and Training. Basic Issues: Policy Implications: How to Promote Transfer*, Research and Development, No. 23, Manpower Services Commission, Sheffield, 1985.

Ansoff, H. I., *Strategic Management*, Macmillan, London, 1979.

Argenti, J., *Practical Corporate Planning*, Geo. Allen & Unwin, London, 1980.

Argyris, C. and Schön, A., *Organisational Learning: A Theory of Action Perspective*, Addison Wesley, Reading, Mass., 1978.

Ausubel, D., 'Cognitive structure and transfer', in *How Students Learn*, eds N. Entwistle and H. Hounsell, University of Lancaster, Lancaster, 1977, pp. 93–104.

Avent, C., 'Transition from school to work', *BACIE Journal*, July/Aug, 1984.

Bales, R. F. *Interaction Process Analysis*, Addison Wesley, Reading, Mass., 1950.

Bank, J., *Outdoor Training for Managers*, Gower Press, Aldershot, 1985.

Baron, B., *Managing Human Resources*, eds A. G. Cowling and C. J. B. Mailer, Arnold, London, 1981.

Barrington, H. A., Continuous development: Theory and reality, *Personnel Review*, 15 (1), 1986, pp. 27–31.

Bass, B. M. and Vaughan, J. A., *Training in Industry – The Management of Learning*, Tavistock Publications, London, 1966.

Becker, H. S., *Outsiders: Studies in the Sociology of Deviance*, The Free Press, New York, 1963.

Belasco, J. A. and Arlutton, J. A., 'Line and staff conflicts: Some empirical insights', *Academy of Management Journal*, 12 Dec. 1969, pp. 469–77.

Belbin, E. and Belbin, R. M., *Problems in Adult Retraining*, Heinemann, London, 1972.

Bennett, R. and Leduchowicz, T., *What Makes for an Effective Trainer?*, MCB University Press Ltd, Bradford, 1983.

Berne, E., *Games People Play: The Psychology of Human Relationships*, Penguin, Harmondsworth, 1976.

Blake, R. R. and Mouton, J. S., *The Versatile Manager: A Grid Profile*, R. D. Irwin, Homewood, Illinois, 1981.

Bloom, B. S., *Taxonomy of Educational Objectives – Cognitive Domain*, Longman, Essex, 1956.

Boddy, D., 'Putting action learning into action', *Journal of European Industrial Training*, 5 (5), 1981.

Boydell, T. H. A., *A Guide to Job Analysis*, British Association for Commercial and Industrial Education, London, 1977.

Boydell, T. H. A., *A Guide to the Identification of Training Needs*, British Association for Commercial and Industrial Education, London, 1983.

Boydell, T. H. A. and Pedler, M., *Managing Self Development: Concept and Practices*, Gower Press, Farnborough, 1981.

Bramham, J., *Practical Manpower Planning*, Institute of Personnel Management, London, 1982.

Bramley, P. and Newby, A. C., 'The evaluation of training: Clarifying the concept', *Journal of European Industrial Training*, 8 (6), 1984.

Brewster, C. and Connock, S., *Industrial Relations Training for Managers*, Kogan Page, London, 1980.

Brief, A. P. and Aldag, R. J., 'Employee reactions to job characteristics: A constructive replication', *Journal of Applied Psychology*, 60, 1975, pp. 182–6.

Brown, W., *Explorations in Management*, Heinemann, London, 1960.

Burgoyne, J. G., 'Moving forward from self development', *Management Education and Development*, 12 (2), 1981, pp. 67–80.

Burgoyne, J. G., 'Management development for the individual and the organisation', *Personnel Management*, June 1988.

Burgoyne, J. G., Boydell, T. and Pedler, M., *Self Development, Theory and Applications for Practitioners*, Assoc. of Teachers of Management, London, 1978.

Burns, T. and Stalker, G. N., *The Management of Innovation*, Tavistock Publications, London, 1966.

Business Review, April 1991.

Business Week, 'Analysis through 1979 and 1980 with the subsequent re-assessment programme', 17 Sept. 1984, pp. 62–8.

Byham, B., 'Assessing employees without resorting to a centre', *Personnel Management*, Oct. 1984.

CNAA (Council for National Academic Awards), *A Feasibility Study on a National Framework of Assessment Arrangements for Management Education*, CNAA, London, 1989.

Cambridge Weekly News, 5 December 1991.

Campbell, J. P., 'On the nature of organisational effectiveness', in *New Perspectives on Organisational Effectiveness*, eds P. S. Goodman, J. M. Pennings and Associates, Jossey-Bass, San Francisco, 1977.

Cannon, J., *Cost Effective Decisions*, Institute of Personnel Management, London, 1979.

Carby, K. and Thakur, M., *Transactional Analysis at Work*, Information Report, No. 23., Institute of Personnel Management, London, 1976.

Carroll, S. J. et al., 'The relative effectiveness of training methods – expert opinion and research', *Personnel Psychology*, 25, 1972, pp. 495–500.

Celinski, D., 'Systematic on the job training', *Training and Development*, Nov. 1986.

Christie, R. and Gers, F. L., eds, *Studies in Machiavellianism*, Academic Press, New York, 1970.

Clutterbuck, D., *Everyone Needs a Mentor*, Institute of Personnel Management, London, 1985.

Clutterbuck, D., 'Managers answer the call for workforce training', *The Times*, 22 Nov. 1990.

Cole, G., 'Management training in top companies', *Journal of European Training*, 5 (4), 1981.

Constable, J. and McCormick, R., *The Making of British Managers*, A report for the BIM and CBI into management training, education and development, April 1987.

Coverdale, R. *The Practice of Teamwork*, Parts I, II and III, Coverdale Organisation.

Crane, S., 'Machiavelli and training', *Personnel Executive*, Sept. 1981.

Cranfield, I., *Training Through Endeavour*, *ICT*, Oct. 1982.

Crofts, P., 'Distance learning's broader horizons', *Personnel Management*, March, 1985.

Dahl, R., 'The concepts of power', *Behavioural Science*, 2, 1957, pp. 201–15.

Daily Mirror, Report on Jasper Carrot, 8 Feb. 1989.

Dalton, M., *Men Who Manage*, John Wiley & Sons, New York, 1959.

de Bono, E., *Lateral Thinking*, home study course, Wolsey Hall, Oxford, n.d.

Department of Employment, *Glossary of Training Terms*, HMSO, London, 1977.

Department of Employment, *Training for employment*, Cmnd 316, HMSO, London, 1988.

Distribution Industry Training Board, *Recommendations on I.R. Training*, DITB, Manchester, n.d.

Dollard, J. and Miller, N.E., *Personality and Psychotherapy: An Analysis on Themes of Learning, Thinking and Culture*, McGraw Hill, New York, 1950.

Donnelly, E. L., *Training as a Specialist Function – An Historical Perspective*, Working Paper Number 9, Faculty of Business Studies and Management, Middlesex Polytechnic, London, 1984.

Donnelly, E. L., The training model: Time for a change? *Industrial and Commercial Training*, 19 (3), 1987.

Downs, S. and Perry, P., 'Can trainers learn to take a back seat?', *Personnel Management*, March 1986.

Drucker, P. F., *Managing for Results*, Harper & Row, New York, 1964.

Drucker, P. F., *The Effective Executive*, Harper & Row, New York, 1967.

Duncan, K. D. and Kelley, C. J., *Task Analysis, Learning and the Nature of Transfer*, Manpower Services Commission, Sheffield, 1983.

Dunlop, J. T., *Industrial Relations Systems*, Holt, New York, 1958.

Easterby-Smith, M. and Tanton, M., 'Turning course evaluation from an end to a means', *Personnel Management*, April 1985.

Edmonds, J., 'A tough line on training', *Personnel Today*, 27 Jun. 1989.

Engineering Industry Training Board, *The Analysis of Certain Engineering Craft Occupations*, research report, no. 2, Engineering Industry Training Board, Watford, 1971.

Engineering Industry Training Board, *Training Officers in the Engineering Industry*, Engineering Industry Training Board, Watford, 1973.

Engineering Industry Training Board, *Review of Craft Apprenticeship in Engineering*, Information Paper, No. 49, Engineering Industry Training Board, Watford, 1978.

Engledow, J. L. and Lenz, R. T., 'Whatever happened to environmental analysis?', *Long Range Planning*, 18, April 1985, pp. 93–106.

Fairbairns, J., 'Plugging the gap in training needs analysis', *Personnel Management*, Feb. 1991.

Fayol, H., *Industrial and General Administration*, trans. J. A. Coubrough, International Management Institute, Geneva, 1930.

Fletcher, C. and Williams, R., *Performance Appraisal and Career Development*, Hutchison, London, 1985.

Fonda, N., 'Management development: The missing link in sustained business performance', *Personnel Management*, Dec. 1989.

Fowler, A., *Getting Off to a Good Start – Successful Employee Induction*, Institute of Personnel Management, London, 1983.

Fox, S. and Smith, D., 'Perspectives in organisational analysis and the management of change', *PR*, 15 (3), 1986.

Frank, H. E., 'The trainer', *Industrial Training International*, 10 (8), 1975.

Frederick, W. G., 'Corporate social responsibility in the Reagan era and beyond', *Calif. Mgt. Review*, 25 (3), 1983.

Freedman, J. L., 'Long term behavioural effects of cognitive dissonance', *Journal of Exp. Soc. Psychol.*, 1, 145–55.

French, J. R. P. and Raven, B. H., 'The bases of social power', in *Studies in*

Social Power, ed. D. Cartright, Ann Arbor, University of Michigan Press, 1959.

Gagné, R., *The Conditions of Learning*, Holt Rinehart & Winston, New York, 1965.

Garbutt, D., *Training Costs with Reference to the Industrial Training Act*, Gee and Company Ltd, London, 1969.

Gilbreth, L. M., *The Psychology of Management*, Sturgis and Walton, New York, 1914.

Glaser, R., *Training Research and Education*, Wiley & Sons, New York, 1965.

Goldstein, I. L., Training in work organisations, *Annual Review of Psychology*, 31, 1980, pp. 229–72.

Grant, D., 'A better way of learning from Nellie', *Personnel Management*, 1984.

Greiner, L. E., 'Evolution and revolution as organisations grow', *Harvard Business Review*, July/Aug. 1972.

Guest, D., 'Personnel and HRM: Can you tell the difference?', *Personnel Management*, Jan. 1989.

HMSO, *Cost Benefit Aspects of Manpower Retraining*, HMSO, London, 1970.

HMSO, *Industrial Relations Code of Practice*, HMSO, London, 1972.

HMSO, *Industrial Relations Training*, HMSO, London, 1972.

HMSO, White Paper *Training for Jobs*, HMSO, London, 1984.

HMSO, *Working Together – Education and Training*, Cmnd 9832, HMSO, London, 1986.

Hackman, J. R., Oldham, G., Janson, R. and Purdy, K., 'A new strategy for job enrichment', *California Management Review*, 15 (3), 1975, pp. 96–7.

Hall, N., *Cost Effective Analysis in Industrial Training*, Manchester Monographs No. 6., University of Manchester, Manchester, 1976.

Hamblin, A. C., *Evaluation and Control of Training*, McGraw-Hill, Maidenhead, 1974.

Handy, C., *The Future of Work*, Basil Blackwell, Oxford, 1984.

Handy, C., *Understanding Organisations*, 3rd edn Penguin Books, Harmondsworth, 1985.

Handy, C., *The Making of Managers*, National Economic Office, London, April 1987.

Harrison, R., 'A new look at the retraining of unemployed executives, *Journal of European Industrial Training*, 1978.

Hayes, C., Anderson, A. and Fonda, N., International competition and the role of competence', *Personel Management*, Sept. 1984.

Hayes, C., Fonda, N., Pope, N., Stuart, R. and Townsend, K., *Training for Skill Ownership*, IMS, Brighton, 1983.

Heller, R., 'The change managers', *Management Today*, 25th Anniversary Issue, 1991.

Hinton, I., 'Learning to manage and managing to learn', *Industrial and Commercial Training*, May/June 1984.

Holding, D. H., *Principles of Training*, Pergamon Press, Oxford, 1965.

Honey, P. and Mumford, A., *Manual of Learning Styles*, Honey, Maidenhead, 1982.

Honey, P. and Mumford, A., *Using Your Learning Styles*, Honey, Maidenhead, 1983.

Howard, J. A. and Sheth, J. N., *The Theory of Buyer Behaviour*, Wiley & Sons, New York, 1969.

Huczynski, A., 'Training methods – fads and fancies?', *British Association for Commercial and Industrial Education Journal*, March/April 1984.

ILO, *Teaching and Training Methods for Management Development*, ILO, Geneva, 1972.

Industrial Society, *Induction* (Notes for Managers No. 21), The Industrial Society, London, 1973.

Industrial Society, *Survey of Training Costs*, New Series No. 1, The Industrial Society, London, 1985.

Industrial Training Research Unit, *CRAMP*, research paper TRI, ITRU n.d.

Industrial Training Research Unit, 'Trainability tests; a practitioner's guide', *ITRU* Research Paper, Cambridge, June 1977.

Institute of Personnel Management, *Interactive Video*, PM Factsheet, ed. C. Hogg, Institute of Personnel Management, London, 1989.

Institute of Personnel Management, *Cotinuous Development: People and Work*, 3rd edn, Institute of Personnel Management, London, 1990.

James, R., 'The use of learning curves', *Journal of European Industrial Training*, 8(7) 1984.

Jennings, S., McCarthy, W. E. J. and Undy, R., *Managers and Industrial Relations: The Identification of Training Needs*, MSC, Sheffield, 1983.

Jennings, S. and Undy, R., 'Auditing managers' IR training needs', *Personnel Management*, Feb. 1984.

Jensen, A. R., *Educability and Group Difference*, Harper & Row, London, 1976.

Johnson, R., 'The case for a training tax', *Personnel Management*, Dec. 1990.

Jones, J. A. G., *Training Intervention Strategies: Making More Effective Training Interventions*, ITS Monograph No. 2, Industrial Training Service Ltd, London, 1983.

Jones, J. A. G. and Moxham, J., 'Costing the benefits of training', *Personnel Management*, 1 (4), 1969.

Jones, M., 'Training practices and learning theories', *JEIT*, 3 (7), 1979.

Kearsley, G. *Costs, Benefits and Productivity in Training Systems*, Addison-Wesley, London, 1982.

Kelly, A. V., *The Curriculum*, Harper & Row, London, 1977.

Kenney, J., 'Core competencies of a trainer', *Canadian Training Methods*, 9 (4) (Supplement), 1976.

Kenney, J. P. J., Donnelly, E. L. and Reid, M. A., *Manpower Training and Development*, Institute of Personnel Management, London, 1979.

Kenney, J. P. J. and Reid, M. A., *Training Interventions*, Institute of Personnel Management, London, 1986.

King, D., *Training Within the Organisation*, Tavistock Publications, London, 1964.

Kolb, D. A., 'Towards an applied theory of experiential learning', in *Theories of Group Processes*, ed. C. L. Cooper, Wiley, New York, 1975.

Kolb, D. A., Rubin, I. M. and McIntyre, J. M., *Organisational Psychology – An Experiential Approach*, Prentice Hall, Englewood Cliffs NJ, 1974.

Koontz, H. and O'Donnell, C., *Principles of Management: An Analysis of Managerial Functions*, international edn, McGraw Hill, Maidenhead, 1968.

Koontz, H., O'Donnell, C. and Weihrich, H., *Management*, 7th edn, International edn, McGraw Hill, Maidenhead, 1980.

Korda, M., *Power! How to Get It*, Random House, New York, 1975.

Kotter, J. P. and Schlesinger, L. A., 'Choosing strategies for change', *Harvard Business Review*, March/April 1979.

Krathwohl, D. R., *Taxonomy of Educational Objectives – Affective Domain*, Longman, Essex, 1964.

Krech, D., Crutchfield, R. S. and Livson, N., *Elements of Psychology* 3rd edn, Knopf, New York, 1974.

Kubr, M., 'Principles for the selection of teaching and training methods', in *Teaching and Training Methods for Management Development*, ILO, Geneva, 1972, p. 3, 1&2.

Labour Relations Agency (N. Ireland), *The Consultative Draft Code of Practice in IR Training*, Labour Relations Agency, N. Ireland, n.d.

Laird, D., *Approaches to Training and Development*, Addison-Wesley, London, 1978.

Lawler, E. E. and Porter, L. W., 'The effect of performance on job satisfaction', in *The Applied Psychology of Work Behaviour*, ed. D. W. Organ, Business Publications, Dallas, Texas, 1978.

Leduchowicz, T., 'Trainer role and effectiveness – a review of the literature, *International Journal of Manpower*, 3 (10), 1982.

Leduchowicz, T. and Bennett, R., *What Makes an Effective Trainer?*, report by Thames Valley Regional Management Centre/Manpower Services Commission, 1983.

Levitt, T., 'Marketing myopia', *Harvard Business Review*, July/Aug. 1960.

Levitt, T., 'Change and business strategy', *Innovation in Marketing*, Pan, London, 1968, p. 17.

Lewis, R. and Margerison, C., 'Working and learning – identifying your preferred ways of doing things', *Personnel Review*, 8 (2), Spring 1979.

Likert, R., *New Patterns of Management*, McGraw-Hill, New York, 1961.

Locke, E. A., 'The ideas of Frederick W. Taylor: An evaluation', *Academy of Management*, Review 7, No. 11, Jan. 1982, pp. 14–24.

Long, C. G. L., 'A theoretical model for method selection', *Industrial Training International*, 4 (11), 1969, pp. 475–8.

Lovelady, L., 'The process of OD: A reformulated model of the change process', *PR*, 13 (2), 1984.

McGregor, D., *The Human Side of Enterprise*, McGraw Hill, New York, 1960.

McMurray, R. N., 'Power and the ambitious executive', *Harvard Business Review*, Nov/Dec. 1973.

Mager, R., *Preparing Instructional Objectives*, Fearon Publishers, San Francisco, 1984.

Mager, R. and Pike, P., *Analysing Performance Problems*, Fearon Publishers, San Francisco, 1970.

Manpower Services Commission, *Training of Trainers*, first report of the Training of Trainers Committee, HMSO, London, 1978.

Manpower Services Commission, *Direct Trainers*, second report of the Training of Trainers Committee, HMSO, London, 1980.

Manpower Services Commission, *A New Training Initiative: An Agenda for Action*, Manpower Services Commission, Sheffield, 1981.

Manpower Services Commission, *Glossary of Training Terms*, 3rd edn HMSO, London, 1981.

Manpower Services Commission, *Looking at Computer Based Training*, Manpower Services Commission, Sheffield, 1981.

Marks, W. R., *Induction: Acclimatising People to Work*, IPM, London, 1970.

Maslow, A. H., *Towards a Psychology of Being*, Van Nostrand, Princeton, 1962.

Massie, J. L., *Essentials of Management*, Prentice Hall, Englewood Cliffs, NJ, 1979.

Megginson, D. and Boydell, T., *A Manager's Guide to Coaching*, British Association for Commercial and Industrial Education, London, 1979.

Miller, V. A., *The Guidebook for International Trainers in Business and Industry*, Van Nostrand Reinhold/American Society for Training and Development, New York, 1979.

Mintzberg, H., *The Nature of Managerial Work*, Prentice Hall, Englewood Cliffs, NJ, 1973.

Mintzberg, H., 'The managers' job – folklore and fact', *Harvard Business Review*, 53 (4), July/Aug. 1975.

Morris, M., 'The evaluation of training', *ICT*, March/April 1984.

Mumford, A., *Making Experience Pay*, McGraw-Hill, Maidenhead, 1980.

Mumford, A., 'Review of action learning in practice', *Industrial and Commercial Training*, 16 (2), 1984.

Mumford, A., 'Self development: missing elements', *Industrial and Commercial Training*, 18 (3), May/June 1986.

NEDO (National Economic Development Office) and MSC (Manpower Services Commission), *Competence and Competition, Training and*

Education in the Federal Republic of Germany, the United States and Japan, NEDO/MSC, London, 1984.

NEDO, *People, The Key to Success*, NEDO, London, 1987.

Nicholson, B., 'Managing change in education and training', *BACIE Journal*, March/April 1985.

Otto, C. P. and Glaser, R. O., *The Management of Training*, Addison-Wesley, London, 1970.

PPITB, *Training Records: An Aid to Sound Company Training*, Training Guide No. 7, PPITB, London, n.d.

Palmer, G., *British Industrial Relations*, Geo. Allen & Unwin, London, 1983.

Parlett, M., 'Evaluating innovations in teaching', in eds H. Butcher and E. Rudd, *Contemporary Problems in Higher Education*, McGraw-Hill, London, 1972.

Parsons, T., *The Social System*, Routledge and Kegan Paul, London, 1951.

Pearson, R., Hutt, R. and Parsons, D., *Education, Training and Employment*, Institute of Manpower Studies Series No. 4, Gower Press, Aldershot, 1984.

Pedler, M., *Action Learning in Practice*, Gower Press, Aldershot, 1983.

Peters, T. J. and Waterman, R. H. (Jr), *In Search of Excellence: Lessons from America's Best Run Companies*, Harper & Row, New York, 1982.

Pettigrew, A. M., Jones, G. R. and Reason, P. W., *Training and Development Roles in their Organisational Setting*, Manpower Services Commission, Sheffield, 1982.

Pettigrew, A. M. and Reason, P. W., *Alternative Interpretations of the Training Officer Role: A Research Study in the Chemical Industry*, Chemical and Allied Products Training Board, Staines, Middlesex, March 1979.

Pettigrew, A. M., Sparrow, P. and Hendry, C., 'The forces that trigger training', *Personnel Management*, Dec. 1988.

Povah, N., 'Using assessment centres as a means for self development', *Industrial and Commercial Training*, March/April, 1986.

RBL, *Research on External and Internal Influences in Training*, report for Manpower Services Commission, Sheffield, The Review Team, Research Bureau Ltd, 1979.

Rackham, N., Honey, P. and Colbert, M., *Developing Interactive Skills*, Wellens Publishing, Guilsborough, 1971.

Reddin, W. K., 'Training and organisational change', *British Association for Commercial and Industrial Education Journal*, 2 (1), March 1968.

Revans, R. W., *The Origins and Growth of Learning*, Bratt, Chartwell, 1982.

Revans, R. W., *The ABC of Action Learning*, Bratt, Chartwell, 1983.

Richardson, J. and Bennett, B., 'Applying learning techniques to on the job development, Part 2', *JEIT*, 8 (3), 1984.

Robbins, S. P., *Organisation Theory: Structure, Design and Applications*, Prentice Hall, New Jersey, 1987.

Robinson, K. R. A., *A Handbook of Training Management*, 2nd edn, Kogan Page, London, 1985.

Robinson, P. J., Faris, C. W. and Wind, Y., *Industrial Buying and Creative Marketing*, Allyn & Bacon, Boston, 1967.

Rodger, A., Morgan, T. and Guest, D., *A Study of the Work of Industrial Training Officers*, Air Transport and Travel Industrial Training Board, Staines, 1971.

Rogers, C., *Freedom to Learn*, Merrill, Columbus, Ohio, 1969.

Rogers, C., *Freedom to Learn for the 80's*, Merrill, Columbus, Ohio, 1983.

Romiszowski, A. J., *The Selection and Use of Instructional Media*, Kogan Page, London, 1974.

Rothwell, S., 'Integrating the elements of a company employment policy', *Personnel Management*, Nov. 1984.

Roy, D. R., 'Banana time: Job satisfaction and informal interaction', *Human Organization*, 18, 1960.

Scarman, L. G., The Brixton Disorders, 10–12 April 1981, *The Scarman Report*, Cmd 8427, HMSO, London, 1981.

Schein, E., *Process Consultation*, Addison-Wesley, Reading, Mass, 1969.

Schein, E., 'Increasing organisational effectiveness through better human resources development', *Sloan Management Review*, 19, 1977.

Schofield, P., 'Outdoor development training', *Personnel Executive*, March 1985.

Seal, J. and McKenna, M., 'British Quality Awards', *The Daily Telegraph*, 8 Nov. 1990.

Seymour, W. D., *Skills Analysis Training*, Pitman, London, 1966.

Shakespeare, W., *Tragedies* (reprint), ed. P. Alexander, Collins, London, 1966.

Silverzweig, S. and Allen, R. F., 'Changing the corporate culture', *Sloan Management Review*, Spring 1976.

Singer, E. J., *Training in Industry and Commerce*, Institute of Personnel Management, London, 1977.

Singer, E. J., *Effective Management Coaching*, Institute of Personnel Management, London, 1979.

Singer, E. J., 'Occupational training families – a breakthrough or a diversion?', *BACIE Journal*, Nov/Dec. 1984.

Skinner, B. F., *Science and Human Behaviour*, Macmillan, New York, 1983.

Sloman, M., 'On the job training – a costly poor relation', *Personnel Management*, Feb. 1989.

Smith, J., Shadow Budget speech, 1990.

Smith, M., 'Using repertory grids to evaluate training', *Personnel Management*, Feb. 1978.

Stake, R. E., 'The countenance of educational evaluation', *Teachers College Record*, 68, 1967.

Stammers, R. and Patrick, J., *The Psychology of Training*, Methuen, London, 1975.

Steele, F., 'Is organisation development work possible in the UK culture?', *Journal of European Training*, 5 (3), 1976.

Stephenson, T., 'OD: A critique', *Journal of Management Studies*, Oct. 1975.

Stewart, A. and Stewart, V., *Tomorrow's Managers Today*, Institute of Personnel Management, London, 1981.

Stoner, J. A. F. and Wankel, C., *Management*, Prentice Hall, New Jersey, 1986.

Stringfellow, C. D., 'Education and training', *Industrial Training International*, 3 (2), 1968.

Stuart, R., 'Using others to learn', *Personnel Review*, 4, 1984.

Stuart, R. and Long, G., 'Towards marketing the training function, Part I', *Personnel Review*, 14 (2), 1985.

Talbot, J. R. and Ellis, C. D., *Analysis and Costing of Company Training*, Gower, Aldershot, 1969.

Taylor, B. and Lippitt, G., *Management Development and Training Handbook*, McGraw-Hill, New York, 1983.

Taylor, F. W., *Scientific Management*, Harper & Bros, New York, 1947.

Teire, J., 'Using the outdoors, *ICT*, March/April 1984.

Thakur, M., Bristow, J. and Carby, K., *Personnel in Change – Organisation Development through the Personnel Function*, Institute of Personnel Management, London, 1978.

Thomason, G., *Textbook of Personnel Management*, Institute of Personnel Management, London, 1981.

Thurley, K. E. and Hamblin, A. C., *The Supervisor and His Job*, HMSO, London, 1963.

Tolman, E. C., *Purposive Behaviour in Animals and Men*, Appleton, New York (originally published 1932), 1967.

Tracey, W. R., *Evaluating Training and Development Systems*, American Management Association, New York, 1968.

Training Agency, *Training in Britain: A Study of Funding Activity and Attitudes*, 4 research reports, HMSO, London, 1989.

Training and Development Lead Body, *How Do You Spot Good Trainers?* consultation document, London, n.d. (circulated 1991).

Training Services Agency, *An Approach to the Training of Staff with Training Officer Roles*, Training Services Agency, Sheffield, 1977.

Turrell, M., *Training Analysis: A Guide to Recognising Training Needs*, Macdonald and Evans, Plymouth, 1980.

University Teaching Methods Unit (UTMU), *Improving Teaching in Higher Education*, UTMU, London, 1980.

Walker, J. W., *Linking HR Planning and Strategic Planning*, unpublished paper to Institute of Management Services, 1977.

Warr, P. B. and Bird, M. W., *Identifying Supervisory Training Needs*, Training Information Paper, No. 2, HMSO, London, 1968.

Warr, P. B., Bird, M. and Rackham, N., *Evaluation of Management Training*, Gower Press, Aldershot, 1970.

Weber M., *Theory of Social and Economic Organisation*, The Free Press, New York, 1947.

White, E. B., *The Creative Writer*, ed. A. M. Mathieu, Writers Digest, Cincinnati, Ohio, 1972.

Williams, A., *Managing Human Resources*, eds A. G. Cowling and C. J. B. Mailer, Arnold, London, 1990.

Winkler, J. T., 'The ghost at the bargaining table: directors and industrial relations', *British Journal of Industrial Relations*, XII (2), 1974.

Wood, R. and Scott, A., 'The gentle art of feedback', *Personnel Management*, March 1989.

Wood, S. J., Wagner, A., Armstrong, E. G. A., Goodman, J. F. B. and Davies, J. E., 'The industrial relations system concept as a basis for theory in industrial relations', *British Journal of Industrial Relations*, XIII, 1975.

Woodward, N., 'A cost benefit analysis of supervisor training', *Industrial Relations Journal*, 6 (2), Summer 1976.

Index